Nsibidi Contemporary Black Playwrights Series ◆ 1

Two Plays of Initiation **by Robert Johnson, Jr**

to the Library of Goshen College

Charles Merrill 2005

(the author's father-in-law)

TWO PLAYS OF INITIATION
Stop and Frisk **and** *The Train Ride*

TWO PLAYS OF INITIATION

Stop and Frisk
and
The Train Ride

Robert Johnson, Jr

Nsibidi
2003

GOSHEN COLLEGE LIBRARY
GOSHEN, INDIANA

Nsibidi Africana Publishers
51, Guilford Road, Milton, MA 02186-4310, USA
Regent House, 291 Kirkdale, Sydenham, London, England, SE26 4QD

First Published January 2003

© Robert Johnson. Jr. 2003

ISBN 0-9722241-8-1

Cover Painting [Untitled] by a Tennessee death-row inmate, Ndume Olatushani {Erskine Johnson}, who maintains that he was wrongfully convicted as a result of illegal police tactics similar to those represented in Robert Johnson, Jr's play, *Stop and Frisk*. Ndume became an accomplished painter while in prison.
Courtesy Robert Johnson, Jr.

All rights reserved.
No part of this publication may be reproduced, stored in or introduced into a retrieval system, or transmitted, in any form, or by any means (electronic, mechanical, photocopying, recording, or otherwise) without the prior written permission of both the above copyright owner and publisher

Cover Design and Typography by Chukwuma Azuonye

Printed in the United States of America

For My Dear Children
**Anika Ama Johnson
& Gary Weldon Johnson**

Other Works by Robert Johnson, Jr.

Scholarly Books

1997. *Shona* (co-edited with Gary N. van Wyk). The Heritage Library of African People. New York: Rosen Publishing Group.
1999. *Why Blacks Left America for Africa.*
2002. *Race, Law, and Public Policy.* 2nd Edition.
In Press *Returning Home: A Century of African-American Repatriation*

Plays

1994. *Freedom's Journeyman.* Premiered as part of Bowdoin College's Bicentennial Celebration, March 4-6. Directed by Nefertiti Burton.
1992. *Mama's Boy.* Premiere Performance by Kenya National Theatre, in February 1972. Directed by Tirus Gathwe.
1991. *Sugar Hill* (co-authored with Amy Merrill). Premiere Performance by Karibu Productions, March 4-April 7. Directed by William Electric Black.

Contents

Stop and Frisk   1

The Train Ride   67

Stop & Frisk
(March, 1993)

Characters

JOHNNIE PETERSON, *20, High School Graduate and Budding Poet.*
EMMA PETERSON, *45, Project Dweller, Johnnie's Mother.*
DORIS MCLELLAN, *35, Homeless Woman, Emma's Friend.*
COPELAND MARSHALL, *Johnnie's Lawyer and Fellow Artist.*
JACOB JONES, *Art Gallery Entrepreneur, Copeland's Friend.*
DARRELL DOBSON, *Crack Cocaine Pusher.*
MIKE CARTER, *Neighborhood Youth.*
JUDGE, *Middle-aged Black Man.*
PROSECUTOR, *White Female.*
COURT OFFICER, *Male or Female.*
POLICEMAN, *White Male.*
POLICEMAN 2, *Black Male.*

The action of the play takes place in and around the City of Boston in the early 1990's.

Donn Swaby as Johnnie Peterson, and Robin Scott Manna as his friend and attorney, Marshall Copeland, in the world premiere of *Stop and Frisk*, directed by James A. Spruill of the New African Company and presented by Karibu Productions at the Strand Theatre, Columbia Road, Dorchester, Massachusetts, on November25-27, 1994. Photo by courtesy of Robert Johnson, Jr.

ACT I

Scene 1

This scene opens in the Orchard Park Housing Project apartment of Emma Peterson, a woman of about forty-five. Her son, Johnnie, 20, is sitting at the kitchen table working on some poems while a tape-recording of Luther Vandross' "So Amazing," is playing in the background. Emma is addressing envelopes.

JOHNNIE. This might be it Ma! *(He starts to read as he turns down the music)* Love is more precious than... *(Thinks to himself)* Than what? *(Prances around the room, then sits down at the table)* Than life? No, no, no. That sounds lame. I got to write something impressive. I want those people at the Artists Collective at my reading tonight, to say: Johnnie Peterson, what a talent! So I got to do better than that.

EMMA. *(Putting envelopes down)* Why don't you write something about these projects?

JOHNNIE. Who wants to hear poems about projects? No. Johnnie Peterson's gonna write about love. Something I know a lot about. You dig. *(Laughs)*.

EMMA. You do. do you? Which of your many girls you gonna write about?

JOHNNIE All of em. But I want you to hear this. When you gonna finish them envelopes? I knew you shouldn't got involved in the tenants' stuff. Look like you got stuck with all the work.

EMMA. Why not. There's a lot to be done around here. This is our home and we got to work to make it better.

JOHNNIE. I know. I know. If we don't take pride in our community, who will? *(Smiles)*.

EMMA. That's right son.

JOHNNIE. Enough of Luther. Let's see how this sounds to John Coltrane. Where's that tape?

EMMA. Don't you lose your father's tape.

JOHNNIE. Why would I do something stupid like that?

Robert Johnson, Jr.   7

EMMA. Just making sure. I'm going in the back to fold some laundry. It's five o'clock. How long you gonna write? You been up all night. You need to rest before you go to that reading. You don't want to be looking all tired. You want to look refreshed as you read them poems about love.

JOHNNIE. I'll rest after I've done my thang. First, I got to run to Dudley to get some more paper. Then I'll put on that new sweater and pants, you bought me.

EMMA. And here, drop these off at the post office. *(She hands him some envelopes)* Make sure you're back soon *(She exits. He gets up and changes the tape to John Coltrane, "You say you care." He sits, listens and begins to read).*

JOHNNIE. *(Reading)* When time is the beginning of the moment of our love. Together, in the arms of our destiny, the embrace of our ecstasy, my love, in the loneliness of my sorrow I wait for you *(He gets back* up) That's it. *(The lights and music slowly fades as he exits).*

Scene II.

This scene opens in Copeland's apartment. While her boy friend, Jacob, is lounging on the couch, drinking wine from a glass, Copeland, a lawyer and an artist, is painting at her easel.

JACOB. Don't you think you should be preparing your statement to the partners' committee?

COPELAND. No. I'm doing exactly what I should be doing right now, painting. How do you like the colors? Too much blue? How about some red and a little yellow? Yellow. Now that really brightens up a canvas. Don't you think?

JACOB. I think you should be getting ready for that meeting. When is it?

COPELAND. A few weeks.

JACOB. You make it sound like it's a year from now.

COPELAND. I'm not worried. I do a good job for that firm. Just last week I billed 80 hours of work. You know how much money that was?

JACOB. A lot. But any young lawyer can rack up hours. You got to make them believe that you want to be a part of the club, that you want to be a partner.

COPELAND. No. Jacob. They only want to know how much money I can bring into the firm. You figure it. Last week they billed me out at $150 an hour. You're smart with numbers. What's that?

JACOB. It's a pretty penny. But frankly. I don't think you are letting them know that this is important to you. When was the last time you had lunch with your managing partner? Last year you didn't go to the firm's Christmas party. This Christmas, you must go. Bring some presents to your boss' wife.

COPELAND. It all sounds quite boring! I get tired of smiling at those dry parties and folks coming up and interrogating me about my life history. Where did you go to school? So what do you do? I feel like saying odd jobs. Now that would be funny, wouldn't it?

JACOB. Yeah, and they'd wonder how you got into the party too. What's wrong with impressing people? Let the white folk see that we've made it too.

COPELAND. My firm makes, on the average. $10,000 a week on my billable hours. What more do they want?

JACOB. That's what I'm trying tell you. You become a partner and you get a piece of a big, lucrative nest egg.

COPELAND. Jacob, I'm not sure I want a piece of that egg.

JACOB. But when you become partner, you'll be an owner. How many black partners are there downtown in the blue chip law firms? You've earned it. You would be the first Black female partner in your firm.

COPELAND. That's nothing to be proud of. Here it is November, 1991, and they can find no other Black lawyers, but me? Now we all over the mail room and they can find us to deliver messages.

JACOB. Haven't you heard, the higher you go up in the atmosphere, the thinner the air becomes. There are no Black galleries on Newbury Street either. Only good galleries, looking for excellent artists, like you.

COPELAND. Why are you bothering me about this law firm stuff

Robert Johnson, Jr.

when I have this show coming up at the collective.

JACOB. You need to be bothered both about your art and about law.

COPELAND. Like I can't handle both. I'm the best lawyer they got. If they don't make me partner, I'll just walk across the street and be their competitor. (*The phone rings*). Who could that be?

JACOB. Your boy friend.

COPELAND. Funny. *(Picks up the phone)* Hello. Yes. This is she. Oh hi. Yes. Where are you? What are you doing there? Uh huh. Yes. Your mother's phone is out. Sure. I'll he there. Sure. It's O.K. I understand. O.K. I'll see you in about an hour.

JACOB. Who was that?

COPELAND. Johnnie Peterson.

JACOB. He had a reading tonight of his poetry. Why didn't he show up?

COPELAND. He's in jail.

JACOB. Jail. What's that all about?

COPELAND. They only gave him one call. He couldn't go into it. A guard was standing nearby.

JACOB. You're not going. We were suppose to spend the evening together.

COPELAND. Another time. Johnnie's a good kid.

JACOB. Then why is he in jail?

COPELAND. I don't know. He sounded upset. The bail is set at $2,000 and he can't get out until it's paid.

JACOB. Maybe I made a mistake in letting him into the collective.

COPELAND. Now don't jump to conclusions. If you want to wait for me, that's fine. It shouldn't take me longer than a couple of hours.

JACOB. I'll wait. You be careful.

COPELAND. You don't have to worry. He's not in the Roxbury jail. He's downtown at Nashua Street. I'll be all right. *(She gets her coat)* I'll see you. (*He hugs her*).

JACOB. Hurry back. You have that painting to finish. I like those bright yellow strokes.

COPELAND. You haven't seen my blue, yellow and red all mixed together.

JACOB. I can't wait.

COPELAND. See you. (*She exits. Jacob walks over to the painting and looks at it as the lights fade*).

Scene III

This scene opens in a holding cell at the county jail. It is a small space with a small table and two chairs. Copeland is seated at the table, going through some papers when Johnnie enters.

COPELAND. Hello Johnnie. Are you O.K.?

JOHNNIE. I'm sorry you have to see me like this, Ms. Marshall.

COPELAND. What happened? A lot of people were waiting to hear your poetry tonight.

JOHNNIE. I had to call somebody, and I knew you were a lawyer. The phone at my house is out. You a criminal lawyer?

COPELAND. No. civil. Sit please. *(Johnnie sits)*

JOHNNIE. I've never been in a place like this. Can you help me?

COPELAND. I don't know yet. My trial experience is with corporate matters. These are serious criminal charges.

JOHNNIE. When am I going to get out of here?

COPELAND. The Bail Commissioner set bail at $2,000.

JOHNNIE. I didn't do nothing. I was sitting across from my house, when the cops started harassing us.

COPELAND. Well. They're charging you with two counts of assault and battery upon police officers and trafficking in cocaine.

JOHNNIE. Cocaine! I didn't have no drugs! I don't use drugs! They assaulted us! They're lying!

COPELAND. Not much can be done about the bail until Monday morning, at court.

JOHNNIE. You mean I got to stay here all weekend?

COPELAND. Unless your people can come up with the bail.

JOHNNIE. My mother's not working. Let me speak to the Bail Commissioner.

COPELAND. He's left for another jail.
JOHNNIE. Can you do me a favor?
COPELAND. Yes.
JOHNNIE. Could you stop by and tell my mom what happened? She'll be scared to death when I don't come home tonight.
COPELAND. I don't think I'm going to stay involved in this case Johnnie. But *(hesitating)* Where do you live?
JOHNNIE. Adams Street. Orchard Park Projects. In Roxbury.
COPELAND. I can't promise you anything. *(She writes)* I have a show next week. I'm painting. I need all my time in the studio, at my easel.
JOHNNIE. I know about your show. And I was going to be there. Do you believe me? We were just sitting there on the steps, talking about girls and old times...

Lights down on this scene and up on the steps of a grocery store that is boarded up. Johnnie, Mike and Darrell are standing out front, talking....

DARRELL. You started school last week?
MIKE. Yeah. This is my last year.
DARRELL. I don't know why you bother. You can't get no job when you get out.
MIKE. Right. But if I quit, Pops will kick my fucking ass. You know what I'm saying?
DARRELL. Your pops ain't having that shit.
MIKE. I was gonna drop out and join the army. But dig this. Uncle Sam don't want you, unless you got a diploma.
DARRELL. Just another way to keep a black man down. What the fuck? You need a high school diploma to carry a gun? There's plenty dudes around here, never got past the eighth grade, who can break a forty-five down and knock a bird outta tree.
MIKE. Yeah, but look who they shooting. Check who's coming here. My man Johnnie. (Johnnie enters, carrying a knapsack) What's up? Cool Breeze. *(Laughing)*.
JOHNNIE. Hey fellas. *(They slap five)* I see you guys still holding

up the corner. What's up. Darrell? Man? What's up?

DARRELL. Same o, Same o.

MIKE. Talking about school and how nothing's happening.

JOHNNIE. Don't let me interrupt. *(He starts going through his bag)*.

MIKE. But I'll graduate, like you man. Try to get a little job doing something.

JOHNNIE. Darrell, you need to get a job.

DARRELL. I got a job.

JOHNNIE. I mean a real job.

DARRELL. You want me to become a plumber, like you. Everybody got to be like you. *(Getting angry)*.

JOHNNIE. Forget it man.

DARRELL. It ain't that easy man. I'm through with school. Don't you think I tried. I can't get a job. They won't hire me man, not even at McDonald's. I thought when I got out of jail, I could start all over. I counted the days until I was released. The first day out, went to all the companies. Couldn't even take the test when they found out about my record.

MIKE. Damn shame. Still paying a debt to society.

DARRELL. That's the problem. Society owes a debt to me.

JOHNNIE. You still talking the same old stuff.

DARRELL. Get real man. All them mother suckers owe me. I spent two and a half years in hell for nothing!

JOHNNIE. You do the crime. You do the time.

DARRELL. Crime? Is it a crime to get in a car on a hot summer day and go for a ride?

MIKE. Nothing illegal about that.

DARRELL. I was sitting on these steps minding my business when some of Joey's boys pulled up in a new Firebird and said let's go to the beach.

MIKE. I remember that summer. It was roasting!

DARRELL. We got as far as the expressway. 5.0 pulled us over. They said the car was stolen. So they hit me with receiving stolen property. Shit, I didn't know it was stolen. I just wanted to go to the beach.

MIKE. You can't go no place in this city without the cops breathing down your back. You walk to Dudley to catch a bus to school, they all over the place. When you get to school, they in front of the building. When you go through the metal detectors, they inside messing with you, because the buzzer goes off. *(Changing the subject, in a reflective mood)* Pops said when he was a kid, they went to City Point to swim.

JOHNNIE. In South Boston?

MIKE. Yeah.

DARRELL. Take your Black ass out there now, and them white folks will drown you. *(Laughs)*.

MIKE. Pops said that's why he never voted for Ray Flynn for Mayor. He said Flynn ain't done a damn thing to desegregate the beaches. Niggers get hot in the summer and the best you can do is jump under a fire hydrant.

DARRELL. Or take a cold shower!

MIKE. *(Changing the subject)* Hey Johnnie. What you so quiet about?

JOHNNIE. Just thinking.

MIKE. About a girl?

JOHNNIE. No. This new poem I been working on. Can't get it right. *(Takes a piece of paper out of his back pocket)*.

DARRELL. We ain't seen you much this summer.

MIKE. He's been hanging out with the white folks. In the rich part of town.

JOHNNIE. The Artists Collective. Why you got to make it a race thang Mike? There's some good people there. Anyway, my English teacher told me to check it out, and she's Black.

DARRELL. Shit man. You just finished high school a few years ago. Sounds like you in love with school.

JOHNNIE. It's not like school.

DARRELL. You get homework?

JOHNNIE. No. People just get together to read their stuff. I'm reading my poems tonight to some important people. *(Lights fade, slow Coltrane, "I Want to Talk About You," plays and his voice can be heard reading poems. Lights back up in the jail interview room)*.

COPELAND. I understand. Everyone was looking forward to your reading.

JOHNNIE. Well. I was ready. Had some new stuff that would have smoked em. Any other Blacks there, but you and Jacob? What's up with that brother anyway? He runs the place. He ought to make sure more of us are there.

COPELAND. *(She stands)* Yes, he has talked about that.

JOHNNIE. There's more. Don't you want to know the rest?

COPELAND. I do. But I must get home.

JOHNNIE. Are you going to represent me? Get me out of here?

COPELAND. I have a show coming up. I will do all I can for you, but I don't know if I can represent you.

JOHNNIE. Do you believe me?

COPELAND. Here is my business card. I'm not making any promises. *(She presses a button to exit the interviewing room. Johnnie looks at the business card as the lights slowly fade and a loud voice can be heard "Johnnie Peterson your visit is over. Please return to your cell").*

Scene IV

The scene opens the next morning in the kitchen of an apartment building. Emma Peterson sits in a drab housecoat drinking coffee. The table is old. There is also a counter with a new coffee percolator, a large old refrigerator and a stove. Emma appears jittery and sits with her head down for most of the tune. Suddenly there is a knock at the door.

EMMA. Who is it? *(Gets up and approaches the door).* Who's there? *(She opens the door and in walks a black woman, about thirty-five, carrying a knapsack).*

DORIS. Let me get to the John. I almost peed on myself on that bus. *(She exists Left. Emma returns to the kitchen and begins to pour DORIS a cup of coffee, Doris re-enters).* How have you been girl? It's getting cold out there. It took me all of twenty minutes to walk here.

EMMA. Oh hi. I thought you were Johnnie. He didn't come in last night. I laid out some new clothes for that poetry reading group and he didn't come home.

DORIS. Johnnie probably met some nice girl and spent the night whispering sweet nothings in her ear. Don't you forget, he's a man now. No little boy no more.

EMMA. I suppose you right. And what kept you this morning? Your bus late? Or you had to stop and talk to everyone.

DORIS. Not everyone, the men. You got to be sociable. Haven't you heard that before. If you want to make it in this world, you got to have a smile and you got to have a little sugar in your bowl. (*Laughs*). You know what I mean? (*Pulling her chair close to Emma*) Yeah, you know Friday night this new guy came into the shelter.

EMMA. Oh no, not another story. I know what you gonna say. He was tall and slim and told you how pretty you are. Save me please. (*She gets up*).

DORIS. I'm serious girl. He is tough. I swear he looks like Billy Dee Williams and Denzel Washington all rolled up into one powerful.

EMMA. Yeah. But I'm worried. It's not like him to stay out all night.

DORIS. Listen, let me tell you about my Buster. What a name!

EMMA. Girl when you gonna learn to leave these good for nothing men alone? How long I known you?

DORIS. Too long it seems. As long as you've been in these here projects.

EMMA. And you ain't changed a lick. First it was Warren who stole every cent you had. Then Marcus.

DORIS. No. No. Leave Marcus out now. (*Laughs*).

EMMA. He was the worst of the bunch.

DORIS. He was sweet, Emma.

EMMA. That was his problem. He was so sweet that you and most of the women around here had to get a taste of him.

DORIS. How was I to know he had other girls. (*Laughing*). You know I'm just a simple young thang from South Carolina.

EMMA. With no sense!

DORIS. You like a big sister to me. Without you, I wouldn't have made it when I came to Boston.

EMMA. You're family!

DORIS. I remember when you met me at the bus station. I had never been on a subway before. I was use to walking down south. We walked everywhere. To the grocery store, to church. In Spartenburg there was nobody left on that piece of a farm, but me.

EMMA. That land had been in your family for a long time. We and everyone else in the town use to come by your Pappy's country store to get fresh meat. Hog mows, pigtails, greens.

DORIS. Yeah, but look what I did. When Pappy died, I worked the farm, paid the hired hand, but the government came right in and took the place. They said for taxes that Pappy never paid. But you know, one of these days I'm gonna go back and look into it. I don't believe them a minute.

EMMA. You know I ain't been back to Spartenburg since Johnnie was born. Can't believe that was twenty years ago. Sometimes I wish I could go back.

DORIS. People know their places. You don't mess with me. I don't mess with you.

EMMA. Until the holidays, then everybody gets friendly. You coming over for Thanksgiving, ain't you?

DORIS. What you think girl? I wouldn't miss that big plate of chittlins for the world..

EMMA. You know I don't cook no hog guts in this house.

DORIS. I know. I'm just playing with you girl.

EMMA. Yeah. It's that time of year again. Ain't it? Before you know, it's Christmas.

DORIS. Christmas in South Carolina. You remember Miss Ann, who my grandmother worked for. She would always pull up this big black Lincoln, with her driver, Pete, and smile this big smile. Now Pete was this tall, black, skinny but cute Negro that we all believed was doing Miss Ann. Course we didn't know for sure. Pete would open the trunk and take out bags full of hand me downs. He would look at me and give me this smile, showing a row of the prettiest white teeth. Girl, he was fine! We would stand there staring at them bags, as Miss Ann would wave her hand, yell Merry Christmas and take off with Pete. Let me tell you, as soon as she was over the hill, we tore into those bags.

EMMA. Her name wasn't Miss Ann. Stop it. You never told me that before. (*Laughing*).

DORIS. It was so help me. Ann Majors. I remember my sister and me fighting over this old fur coat. We fought all day, Christmas. But that stopped real quick. My father took the coat and gave it to an old lady down the road and gave us the worst whipping of our lives.

EMMA *(Changing the subject)* I sent the letters out to the tenants.

DORIS. Yeah (*Standing up and going to the refrigerator*) I know you got something in here. (*She opens the door and exposes a full refrigerator*). Look a here.

EMMA. Are you eating again?

DORIS. No, I was with him.

EMMA. And him keeps you away from food. Who is he anyway?

DORIS. Buster! I told you already.

EMMA. Does he work?

DORIS. Not yet. But he'll find one. He's out there every morning, looking as soon as he gets off the bus. Sometimes he gets day work. Emma he's real cute and nice.

EMMA. How come he ain't been working and living at a shelter?

DORIS. Just got out of jail. (*Looking at the clock on the wall*). Oh that reminds me. I got to go. I got to meet him at 9:30.

EMMA. I thought you wanted something to eat. And I haven't let me tell you about Johnnie.

DORIS. Tomorrow morning. I saw those sausages in there. Maybe we can knock off some eggs, biscuits, sausages and grits. (*Puts on her coat*).

EMMA. If you can find the time! I got things to do too. You usually get here about 7:30 and we have coffee.

DORIS. And breakfast. And that won't change. But Buster and me gonna look for jobs together. Today we gonna do Boylston Street. Stop in every store! Being homeless ain't gonna lick me.

EMMA. You know you're welcome here. I don't care what the housing authority says, you can come back here. We having a meeting. And we got two hundred names on our petition for a tenant's association. You don't have to stay out in those streets.

DORIS. I know that. And I appreciate you. But I got to try to do something for myself. You know, before you know it, it's seven o'clock and back on the smelly bus. And it won't wait for nobody. If you ain't in that line, it leaves with someone else in your place. There's always someone to take your place in that line.

EMMA. I'm just trying to say.

DORIS. Say what? You don't have to worry about me. I got friends out there too. They take care and look out for me.

EMMA O.K., I'll see you later. Then we'll have breakfast tomorrow. (*Pointing to the refrigerator*) It's full and waiting for you.

DORIS. Definitely tomorrow morning. (*Doris takes Emma in her arms and embraces her.*) I'll see you. And Johnnie will show up. Remember, he's a man now. (*They exit*).

EMMA. Be careful. (*She exits stage, lights remain up and a Luther Vandross song, "The Second Time Around," starts to play. She returns to the kitchen, takes out a skillet, then sits down to her cup of coffee. The music plays for about two minutes when there is a loud knock at the door. She gets up, goes to the door and lets two people enter.*)

COPELAND. Hi, Ms. Peterson. I'm Copeland Marshall. This is Jacob Jones, a friend of mine.

EMMA. What can I do for you?

COPELAND. Your son is Johnnie Peterson? Is that right?

EMMA. Where is he? Is he in trouble?

COPELAND. Yes, he is. I talked to him last night.

EMMA. What kind of trouble? Let me go turn this music down. Have a seat. Where is my child?

COPELAND. He's in jail.

EMMA. Oh my God! No! No! No! In jail for what?

COPELAND. The police arrested him on Adams Street and they are charging him with trafficking in cocaine.

EMMA. What! They got the wrong boy. You know that. Don't you? He's starting plumbing school next week.

COPELAND. The police are saying he was arrested with two other boys, who had drugs on them.

EMMA. Then why don't they let my boy go?

COPELAND. I agree with you. But the law sees it a little differently.

EMMA. (*In a soft voice*) It always does when it comes to us.

COPELAND. I know how you feel, but the charges are very serious and from the little research I've done, if he is convicted he could get a mandatory five years.

EMMA. Five years? That child ain't never been in no trouble. When he see the judge?

COPELAND. First there's a bail hearing Monday morning. If bail is given, then he can get out until trial.

EMMA. How much is his bail gonna be?

COPELAND. It's hard to say. The Bail Commissioner has set it at $2,000.00. The Judge could make it whatever he wants.

EMMA. How long you been a lawyer? Is he gonna help you on this case? (*Pointing to Jacob*).

COPELAND. Mam, he's not a lawyer. And I don't know if I can help Johnnie. I'm not a criminal lawyer.

EMMA. And my child is no criminal!

COPELAND. Ms. Peterson, I've never done a criminal case.

EMMA. So you just gonna drop him now. I don't have no money for a lawyer.

COPELAND. My firm may not let me represent him.. Now how much money can you come up with? Do you have two thousand dollars.

EMMA. Do I look like I got two thousand dollars?

COPELAND. I'm just asking you in case the judge keeps it at $2,000.

EMMA. If I can't afford a lawyer, I can't afford bail.

COPELAND. I agree, but, we have to put up some money to get Johnnie out.

EMMA. I got one thousand dollars in there. Five hundred and fifty is for the rent. I ain't been working for the past five years. I'm on SSI. Disability. That's why I'm here in public housing. Doctors say I can't work. Disabled.

COPELAND. I understand.

EMMA. You mean they will keep my boy in there for something he didn't do simply because I ain't got no money to give them?.

COPELAND. Yes, mam.

EMMA. You get the bail down to five hundred dollars. Can you do that?

COPELAND. I must check with my firm.

EMMA. Where's your firm?

COPELAND. Downtown.

EMMA. That's all you can say. (*Raising her voice*) What you come here for?

JACOB. Ms. Peterson you are not being fair to Copeland.

EMMA. You not a lawyer. Your son ain't sitting in some jail where he ain't suppose to be. You ain't got nothing to say on this.

JACOB. I'm just saying you should give her a chance to help your son. She's only been on the case one day.

EMMA. You got no right to speak on this.

JACOB. I'm just trying to help.

EMMA. The only help I need from you is to talk to those folks downtown and tell them to release my baby. Can you do that? If you can't then you can't do a thang for me.

JACOB. (*Angry*) Copeland, let's get out of here!

COPELAND. Wait Jacob. (*Taking his arm*) Ms. Peterson. I understand your frustration. All of us at the collective have grown fond of Johnnie. He and I have developed a special friendship.

EMMA. My son needs legal help, not friendship.

COPELAND. I've read some of his poems. They are quite good.

EMMA. And we don't need no pity either.

COPELAND. Ms. Peterson. I didn't have to go to the jail, then come here. But he asked me to come and tell you about his arrest. It was late last night when I left the jail, so I came early this morning.

EMMA. Well, I appreciate it. How would I have known? What kind of drugs?

JACOB. Crack. And let's go Copeland. I've heard enough! (*Takes Copeland by the arm*).

EMMA. That's the problem. They think all Black boys are selling crack. All I hear is crack, crack, crack. I never hear about white folks being arrested for this stuff. Why don't they arrest those big men who bring it into the country?

COPELAND. Before I leave I must tell you. The state is going to try to make a case that the drugs were found in the projects.

EMMA. I thought they were arrested on Adams Street in front of the

Robert Johnson, Jr.

old store. That's not in the projects.

JACOB. Big deal!

EMMA. But that's not the projects. That's across the street from the projects.

COPELAND. Stay out of this Jacob. I agree with Ms. Peterson, but I'm just telling you what they are going to try to prove. That he and the other boys were selling drugs in the projects.

EMMA. Then they'll throw me out in the streets.

COPELAND. They have no right to evict you. You must fight them..

EMMA. Doris fought them too. But they threw her out like trash. You know what that feels like? It gnaws at you, right here—deep inside. (*Pointing to her stomach*) You feel like you have no place here, that you happened to just be born into this hell... to be white folk's trash.

JACOB. Try to see it differently. Not all whites are your enemy. I accepted Johnnie into the collective after a white member told me he was a good poet. You got to try a little harder than that.

EMMA. Try! What you think I been doing? I worked all my life, till I got hurt in that cigar factory. That's when I learned what lawyers are all about. I got a little over half of my weekly wage. That's $165. I couldn't pay $650 a month in rent and eat and take care of my child on what I got. And I can't go back to work either because of the pain that shakes my body almost constantly.

JACOB. There are a lot of people pulling for Johnnie. Copeland got involved yesterday as soon as we heard that he had been arrested. We are here even on the weekend, trying to help your son.

EMMA. Ms. Copeland you better get him out of here and fast!

COPELAND. The hearing is Monday. Nine a.m. Superior Court. Seventh Floor.

EMMA. I'll be there. And thanks for coming to tell me.

COPELAND. You are welcome. And bring the bail money.

EMMA. I'll be there bright and early.

JACOB. I'll be seeing you Ms. Peterson.

EMMA. Will you be at the Court tomorrow?

JACOB. No, I got to get back to work.

EMMA. What do you do?

JACOB. I own several art galleries on Newbury Street.

EMMA. Pardon me. I see some folks are moving up in the world. So long, Ms. Copeland and please help us. (*She ushers them to the door.*)

COPELAND. Good-bye (*They exit. Emma goes back to kitchen, pours herself another coffee and sits. Luther Vandross' "The Second Time Around," begins as the lights slowly fade*).

Scene V

The scene opens in a court room. At stage left and upstage is a podium and directly in front of it are two benches with four chairs at each bench. Behind these two benches is a wooden bar. At the rear of the stage is a long bench. As the scene opens Copeland, Doris and Emma are hovered at the long bench speaking softly. A court officer, dressed in uniform stands at the front of the courtroom. A white female, the Prosecutor, stands at the front table.

COURT OFFICER. Court. (*In a loud voice*) All stand please. (*The Judge, who is Black, enters dressed in a black robe. After the Judge sits, the Court Officer speaks*) Be seated please.

JUDGE. It is my understanding that we have some bail petitions.

PROSECUTOR. Yes, your honor. They should be bringing the prisoners down any minute. (*As he ends his statement, three Black men in chains, Johnnie, Darrell and Mike, are led in by a Court Officer and sit in the bench at the rear of the stage*).

JUDGE. You may begin.

PROSECUTOR. Thanks your honor. This is a bail petition from the lower court. There are three co-defendants, each charged with trafficking in class B substance, cocaine.

JUDGE. Was it crack cocaine?

PROSECUTOR. Yes your honor.

JUDGE. Where were they arrested?

PROSECUTOR. At Orchard Housing Project.

COPELAND. I beg your pardon. It was on a public street and not in the project.

JUDGE. Please don't interrupt your sister. You will have your turn.

COPELAND. I apologize your honor.

JUDGE. You may continue (*Pointing to the PROSECUTOR*).

PROSECUTOR. As I said they were arrested at the project and fifty grams of cocaine was found on their persons.

JUDGE. There's a mandatory here?

PROSECUTOR. Yes, and the Commonwealth has a strong case.

JUDGE. Since it's their petition, let me hear first from the defense. Ms. Marshall?

COPELAND. Thanks your honor. For the record, my name is Copeland Marshall and I represent Johnnie Peterson. Your honor, contrary to what my sister has said, my client was not arrested in the projects, but in the public streets.

JUDGE. But what difference does it make counselor?

COPELAND. The state is going to try to prove that the defendants were engaged in a drug transaction in the projects so that they can be evicted by the housing authority.

JUDGE. That might be so, but what does that have to do with this court?

COPELAND. Plenty. The family becomes homeless.

JUDGE. That's not my concern. This is a bail petition, nothing more. I think you would serve your client better if you confined your remarks to the issues before this court.

COPELAND. Yes, your honor. Your honor, Mr. Peterson was born in Boston. He is now age twenty. He lives with his mother, Emma Peterson, who is in the court today, along with her friend. Mr. Peterson attended English High School and graduated this year. He is scheduled to start plumbing school in September. He's a poet. He was an average student and has never been in trouble with the law. The family lives in Orchard projects. He is the only child of Ms. Peterson. He tells me that on the night in question, he was coming home from a basketball game when he was approached by two young men sitting with him in the court. He tells me that he knew the two young men from the neighborhood but did not hang out with them. He tells me that as he walked with them one offered him a beer and they sat down in front of an abandoned store and started to talk about old times in the projects. He tells me that he talked about old times in the neighborhood. He tells me he talked for about a half an hour when the police pulled up in front of them, got out of the car and started searching them. Your honor there was no reason for the search of these young men. They were not committing any crimes. They were just sitting there.

PROSECUTOR. They were in a high crime area your honor.

COPELAND. High crime. This was their home. They were where they were supposed to be. Is it unlawful for a person to be born poor and happen to reside in a certain neighborhood?

JUDGE. It is relevant to the question of the officer's reasonable suspicion. Counselor, isn't that something that should be the subject of a motion to suppress?

COPELAND. I believe it is important now as well, your honor. These boys were just sitting in their neighborhood and the police searched them for no reason, without any probable cause. They are protected by the United States Constitution from unreasonable searches and seizures.

JUDGE. This is not appropriate in this hearing, counselor. I'm not going to warn you again.

COPELAND. But the court must consider whether it will compound an injustice by further restricting these young men's freedom. This is not a police state.

JUDGE. Young lady, that is it. One more unreasonable statement by you and I will hold you in contempt of court. Do you understand what I'm saying? This is your last chance. This is not a motion to suppress. This is a hearing for bail. Do you understand?

COPELAND. Yes. But would this court allow police in South Boston to just randomly search young men who are just sitting.

JUDGE. That's it. I will see you in my chambers at the conclusion of this hearing. I have warned you to stick to the issues before the court.

COPELAND. These are the issues.

JUDGE. What does South Boston have to do with this case? You think about that because you better have a good answer.

COPELAND. Yes, your honor. The police searched the young men. They found no drugs on my client. They found no drug paraphernalia on him. They found no large sums of money on him. In fact, they only found $1.25 on him. His mother has told me that she can come up with $500.00 for bail. As the court knows, the purpose of bail is to insure that a defendant will return to trial. This young man has no prior convictions or any history of defaults. He has strong roots in this community. His mother tells me that he has no other relatives, so it is unlikely that he will flee to another state. He has no money to go anywhere. He is a safe risk. He will return to trial. I therefore ask that his bail be set at $500.

JUDGE. Thanks Ms. Marshall. The Commonwealth wants to be heard?

PROSECUTOR. Yes we would. Your honor. The police seized from these young boys over fifty grams of crack cocaine.

COPELAND. Objection.

JUDGE. Please don't interrupt.

PROSECUTOR. That is a large seizure. The seizure occurred in an area that is heavily populated by young children and in fact there is a school a few blocks away.

COPELAND. Objection.

JUDGE. Overruled.

PROSECUTOR. The boys were searched in a high crime area. The police will testify at trial, and are available this morning, that the boys had been under surveillance and that they had received information from an informant that a gang of young people in the projects was controlling the crack cocaine trade.

COPELAND. Objection to the use of the term gang. There's no evidence of gang activity. These were just young men sitting on a stoop in their neighborhood.

JUDGE. Overruled. You may continue. And I may want to hear from those officers.

PROSECUTOR. Yes, your honor. The arresting officers are here. The neighbors have been constantly calling the police. They are afraid to go out of their apartments day and night. The police instituted a surveillance program in the projects and used extensive informants. The situation has gotten out of control.

COPELAND. Objection, your honor. Crime has nothing to do with my client, your honor. He just happens to live there, be black and eighteen. This young man has no prior record.

JUDGE. There's always the first time. A record has a beginning and it appears that this young man has begun his.

COPELAND. Respectfully, the court has missed my point.

JUDGE. No, I got your point, counselor. Now I want you to get mine. Do you have a recommendation for the Court (*Pointing to the Prosecutor*).

PROSECUTOR. I ask the court to set the bail at two thousand dollars.

JUDGE. (*Pointing to Copeland*) What do you say?

COPELAND. Five hundred dollars. That's all this family can raise. The mother is here. She is disabled, not working. Five hundred dollars to this family is like ten thousand dollars.

JUDGE. (*Interrupting*) Well, before I decide, let me hear from an officer. Who is the officer?

PROSECUTOR. Officer O'Connell. (*The Court Officer exits and returns with a white Police Officer. The officer takes the stand*).

COURT OFFICER. Do you swear to tell the truth, the whole truth and nothing but the truth, so help you God?

POLICE OFFICER. I do.

PROSECUTOR. Please state your name for the record.

POLICE OFFICER. Officer Tom O'Connell.

PROSECUTOR. Officer, I would like to call your attention to September 27, 1992 and ask if you were on duty that day.

POLICE OFFICER. Yes, at about 4:30. I was on routine patrol near the corner of Massachusetts Avenue and Washington Street.

PROSECUTOR. Did you make some observations officer?

POLICE OFFICER. Yes. I noticed a young black man on the island on Massachusetts Avenue acting peculiar. I pulled the cruiser next to him. I was on Massachusetts Ave. going in the direction of City Hospital. I stopped, got out of the cruiser, asked him for identification, at which point he said that he didn't have any. I then asked him to get in the cruiser because I had received a radio call earlier that a young black man had robbed a grocery store in the neighborhood fifteen minutes earlier. He got into the cruiser. I started to search him when all of a sudden he kicked me in the stomach, causing me to fall backwards. I gained my balance, held onto his coat as he continued to strike me with his left hand. He pulled as I tried to get a firm grip on him and finally slipped out of the jacket and ran up Washington Street and down Northampton Street.

PROSECUTOR. Do you see that person in the court room today?

POLICE OFFICER. Yes, he's sitting over there in the blue shirt.

PROSECUTOR. May the record reflect that the officer has identified the defendant, Johnnie Peterson.

JUDGE. The record may so reflect. Would the defense like to cross-examine the witness?

COPELAND. Yes, your honor. Officer. When you stopped the black youth on Massachusetts Avenue, it was getting dark? Wasn't it?

POLICE OFFICER. Yes.

COPELAND. And the only description that you had of the person who allegedly robbed a grocery store was that he was a young black male, isn't that right?

POLICE OFFICER. Yes.

COPELAND. You didn't find any large sums of money on Mr. Peterson, did you?

POLICE OFFICER. No.

COPELAND. He was not identified by any employees at the grocery store as the person who had robbed the store?

POLICE OFFICER. No.

COPELAND. In fact you have no witnesses whatsoever who would put Mr. Peterson in the grocery store?

POLICE OFFICER. That is right.

COPELAND. When that young black man on Massachusetts Ave. got away from you, you were angry weren't you?

POLICE OFFICER. No.

COPELAND. You mean to tell this court that you were not angry that a suspect, whom you had in your custody, in your cruiser, got away. Is that what you want this court to believe?

POLICE OFFICER. OK. I was upset.

COPELAND. Because you had apprehended many suspects in the past. And you had been trained in how to apprehend suspects. Isn't that correct?

POLICE OFFICER. Yes, I was upset and I felt bad that he had got away.

COPELAND. And he got away from you in a busy intersection? There's a lot of traffic in that intersection? A lot of businesses.

POLICE OFFICER. Yes.

COPELAND. None of the people in that busy intersection are here in court today to identify Mr. Peterson as the person who got away from you. Isn't that right?

POLICE OFFICER. Right.

COPELAND. In fact, you never interviewed anyone at that intersection to find out if they could identify Mr. Peterson as the person who got out of your cruiser. Isn't that correct?

POLICE OFFICER. Correct.

COPELAND. I have no further questions.

JUDGE. Does the prosecution have any further questions?

PROSECUTOR. No. The prosecution has established that it was a high crime area. The police were doing their job to protect law-abiding people.

JUDGE. The bail is four thousand dollars. This court is adjourned. Young lady, I'll see you in my chambers. (*He gets up and leaves*).

COURT OFFICER. All rise. This court is adjourned. (*He leads Johnny and the others out of the court. As he passes by her, Emma cries out*).

EMMA. My baby. No, my baby. (*Doris hugs her. The lights fade out slowly*).

Scene VI

This scene opens in the Judge's chambers. As the lights come up, the Judge is getting out of his robe.

JUDGE. Sit please. *(Looking at Copeland)* That was quite a spectacle out there, counselor.

COPELAND. I'm sorry. I didn't know it would go this way.

JUDGE. I understand that you're from the firm of Smith, Child and Smith. Down on State Street you may run things a little different, but up here in my court, I give the orders. Do you understand me?

COPELAND. Yes, but I was only trying to.

JUDGE. Whatever you were trying to do, you did not do a good job. Now *(Turning to the PROSECUTOR)*. What are you going to do with this case?

PROSECUTOR. We plan to try the three of them and get the mandatory.

JUDGE. *(Turning to Copeland)* You hear that? You want to risk big time or would your client take a plea?

COPELAND. He wants a trial. He's innocent.

JUDGE. They all say that. They look at too much T.V., too much Perry Mason, or that new show. Is Perry Mason still on the air? *(Looking at the Prosecutor)*.

PROSECUTOR. I think it is, your honor. At night. Late at night.

JUDGE. Well, if he wants a trial, that's what he will get. *(Looking through his desk drawer)* You ladies mind if I have a cigar? I don't seem to have any left.

PROSECUTOR. Try one of these. *(She hands him a lolly pop)*.

JUDGE. Thanks. Are you ready for trial, Ms. Marshall?

COPELAND. No. I mean, not yet.

JUDGE. She's one of the best in the District Attorney's Office.

COPELAND. I'm very much aware of her reputation.

JUDGE. Then, I will see you again soon. And counselor do us all a favor, have a big long talk with your people.

COPELAND. Yes sir, I will do that.

JUDGE. I don't like the idea of holding you in contempt of my court.

COPELAND. Neither do I.

JUDGE *(Looking at Prosecutor)* And before I forget, when are you going to bring the other two back, since we didn't get a chance to complete everything this morning.

PROSECUTOR. This afternoon.

JUDGE. Good. I want to run out and get me a box of Davidoffs. You know what they are Ms. Marshall?

COPELAND. Very expensive cigars.

Stop and Frisk

JUDGE. Not just your every day run of the mill expensive cigars. But the best outside of Cuba. Dominican and hand made.

COPELAND. Your honor, I don't... (*Interrupted by Judge*).

JUDGE. Good night counselors. (*They exit as he sits back in his seat sucking the lolly pop as the lights fade*).

Scene VII

This scene opens at Emma's apartment. It is in the afternoon. Emma and Doris are sitting in the kitchen. Luther Vandross' ("Second Time Around") is playing in the background as the two begin to talk.

DORIS. That judge didn't give a damn honey. He thinks because he got that black robe on that his shit don't.

EMMA. He had his mind made up. He wasn't gonna let Johnnie go.

DORIS. That's the problem with our people. They get a little education.

EMMA. And a little power.

DORIS. And they think they white.

EMMA. It's a damn shame. You catch hell from Mr. Charlie and from what they call em?

DORIS. Tom.

EMMA. That's it. Uncle Tom.

DORIS. Well I wish I had something to give you for the bail money.

EMMA. I just appreciate you coming.

DORIS. I told Buster, we had to do it another time, not this morning, cause I had to be with my girl.

EMMA. Thanks. I know you were looking for jobs.

DORIS. You know we walked. Oh! I didn't tell you what happened on Boylston Street.

EMMA. Did you find a job?

DORIS. I think Buster might have something. You see we had walked all morning. Going up stairs and filling out applications. It takes half an hour to fill out one of those things. Then this one lady. A Miss Ann at a shoe store. She had the nerve to ask for a. What they call it. I wrote it here. (*She goes in her pocket and takes out a piece of paper*). Here it is—a resume.

EMMA. What's that?

DORIS. Damn if I know. Oh yeah. I got a scratch card. Here. Digs into her pocket. You ever play Royal Flush?

EMMA. No. Just another gimmick to get your money.

DORIS. No. I made $50 two months ago. Been playing it ever since, a dollar a day, sometimes two dollars if Buster gets a few dollars. Here you got a pencil.

EMMA. There's one over near the coffee pot.

DORIS. (*She walks over to the counter and takes up the pencil and begins to scratch the card*). Let me see if this is my lucky day. (*She scratches*). Nothing on that. Three more (*She scratches again*) Damn nothing.

EMMA. Lady, Luck don't seem to be coming this way no time soon. (*She drops her head on the table*).

DORIS. (*Going over to her*) Cheer up, sis. Everything will work out. You'll see. Here, come on, let's dance to a little Luther. (*She changes the tape and puts on "Having a Party" and starts to dance.*).

EMMA. No Doris. Not today. Luther can't make it today. (*Cuts music off*) But you know how that made me feel this morning, seeing my child come into that courtroom in chains. It went all the way to the pit of my stomach. I cried all morning after you left. I just couldn't stop. I would dry my eyes and try to think about something else, but the tears just kept coming. They didn't have to have him in chains like that.

DORIS. Like a slave.

EMMA. But we'll be nobody's slave.

DORIS. Not your Johnnie. The boy is smart. Been writing them poems since he was a kid.

EMMA. Promised me he wouldn't end up like his father Big John, dead. I knew something was wrong when he started playing Big John's music the other day.

DORIS. Johnnie'll come out of this all right.

EMMA. Big John was a stubborn man, always looking to tackle the things he had no business messing with.

DORIS. I know what happened. You don't have to talk about it.

EMMA. The police never did a damn thing about it.

DORIS. He was shot by a white man. What you expect? You don't have to talk about it. Why don't I put on some more Luther?

EMMA. I ain't in a Luther mood right now? My child's in jail. (*EMMA gets up and runs to each wall of the room and starts to push at them as if trying to move them.*).

DORIS. What are you doing Emma? Are you O.K.?

EMMA. No. I'm not! I'm tired! I'm tired! I raised my son to do the right thing! And I prayed everyday that I would not have to bury my only child. I'm tired of going to funerals. Two last week for neighbor's kids, Now this! I have no one!

DORIS. You have me. You can depend on me.

EMMA. Can I Doris? When you came to me, with no place to stay, you stayed here with us. I gave you Johnnie's bed, and he slept on the floor.

DORIS. I appreciated that, sis.

EMMA. Then the project people threw you out because they said you were not a relative. I gave you money for that lawyer, remember?

DORIS. Of course I remember.

EMMA. And you been coming here for breakfast for four months since you been in the shelter, right?

DORIS. Yeah, but what's the point?

EMMA. The point is, I'm tired of listening to your talk about Buster. I need someone to listen to me. I need more than that!

DORIS. Emma, don't talk about needs. I have plenty of them too. At least you got Johnnie. Who do I have?

EMMA. Buster.

DORIS. Yeah, but when I try to share with you what good things are happening, you get mad.

EMMA. I'm not mad! I just get tired! tired! You understand. Everywhere I look someone is trying to tear me down. I try to take one step forward, they knock me back two.

DORIS. But I'm not knocking you back. I'm trying to be your friend.

EMMA. Then talk to me. I don't want to hear about Buster! I want you to talk to me. Do you understand what I'm saying?

DORIS. I understand you're putting pressure on me *(Starts to cry)*.

EMMA. Pressure?

DORIS. You want me to do what you say?

EMMA. What? What you talking about?

DORIS. That's the way people are. They want you to jump here! Jump there! Jump all around the place. I ain't jumping no more. I ain't *(She cries louder and heads for the door)*. I'm tired of jumping around for everybody.

EMMA. I didn't mean it that way. Doris you don't have to leave.

DORIS. Yes I do!

EMMA *(Grabs Doris)*. Please don't go. You don't have to leave! I'm sorry.

DORIS. You want to take the rest of the day from me. You want me to be cramped up in this place, like you.

EMMA. That's not what I want.

DORIS. Oh yes it is, you want me to dry up like you, but I won't!

EMMA. Don't leave. You don't have to go.

DORIS. Yes I do! You think this apartment is gonna protect you. I may not have a place of my own, but every morning, I'm looking, searching, moving from block to block, sitting in the parks, looking at life. You won't stop me, and you can't keep me here. (She *exits)*.

Scene VIII

The scene opens at Copeland's home. She is working at her easel when there is a knock at the door. Doris enters.

DORIS. Hi. Can I come in for a minute.

COPELAND. You sounded urgent on the telephone.

DORIS. Thanks for letting me come over.

COPELAND. Please come in. Have a seat.

DORIS. I won't stay long. I'm worried about my friend, Emma.

COPELAND. How is she doing? I'm sorry about what happened in court. This is my first criminal case.

DORIS. It wasn't your fault. I've seen it happen many times before.

COPELAND. You been before that Judge?

DORIS. No. But I been in other courts. You been in one, you been in em all. With friends, of course.

COPELAND. What can I do for you? I have some painting to do.

DORIS. You paint watercolors?

COPELAND. No. Oils.

DORIS. I know you busy, but Emma is my best friend. When I came here, she took me in. She like the only family I have. And she only has me and Johnnie. Now Johnnie been taken away and she don't quite know what to do. This morning Emma and me had our first fight. I said things to her that was mean. Then I walked out on her. She has no one Ms. Copeland. And she's a good person. She raised Johnnie to be a good boy. Can you try to help again?

COPELAND. (*A little embarrassed*) Would you like some white wine?

DORIS. I never heard of such. Now it really ain't white?

COPELAND. No. It isn't. It's just a figure of speech.

DORIS. (*Laughing*) I know. I know. I'll take a little white wine. Just a little bit, Cause I know you busy. I only drink a little from time to time. For my arthritis, you know.

COPELAND. Yes, (*She pours*) I tried in that courtroom and you see what happened. It made no difference.

DORIS. Can you try again, Ms. Copeland? If Johnnie is sent away, we all be in that cell.

COPELAND. I do have a show coming up soon. But, I know how important this case is to you and Emma.

DORIS. I saw you in that courtroom. You talk like you know what you talking about. And you ain't afraid. (*Looking around the room*). Maybe I should not have come. You have a lot of important things to

Robert Johnson, Jr.   35

tend to. This is a very nice place. (*She drops her head*).

COPELAND. Doris. I will see Emma.

DORIS. You will! You're something special.

COPELAND. And so are you.

DORIS. I must go now. Bye. And thanks!

COPELAND. You're welcome. (*Doris exits. Copeland walks slowly around the room, when there is a knock*) Who could this be? Did she leave something? (*She opens the door and sees Jacob*). Hi. I didn't expect you. (*He enters*).

JACOB. I must talk with you.

COPELAND. Not now.

JACOB. It can't wait! People at the collective were talking about what happened in court. Since you didn't come in, I wanted to come over and talk with you.

COPELAND. So talk.

JACOB. I'm sorry for how things went the other day. I should have gone to court to support you. It's just that this Johnnie stuff came up at the wrong time.

COPELAND. I didn't ask for it either.

JACOB. What I was trying to say the other night is that if I lived in a place like that, I would be getting up early and staying up late to make sure I could get out.

COPELAND. Well, good for you.

JACOB. You can't go much further back than that. Your back's against the wall. You got to go forward.

COPELAND. Don't you think they know it.

JACOB. I'm just saying that they can do better. You heard Ms. Peterson. The first thing that came out of her mouth was this stuff about white people.

COPELAND. And you didn't understand what she was saying?

JACOB. No. I didn't. Blaming white people didn't get me where I'm at.

COPELAND. And where are you at?

JACOB. Look, I went to state college in New York City. Borrowed

$10,000 against an insurance policy my father left me. With that money I started a cleaning company, hired a bunch of emigrants.

COPELAND. I've heard the story.

JACOB. I worked for what I got. I hustled. I begged until I got this New York City cleaning contract, then others from the major corporations. I didn't go in there with my hat in my hand. I went in there, sat down at the big table, looked the man straight in the eye and said, I can do this job for you.

COPELAND. Why are you going over this again. Can't you see I'm trying to paint.

JACOB. I made millions when I sold the company. Moved to Beacon Hill. Started the collective.

COPELAND. And you hope to discover new talent and make even more millions. (*Angrily*) I've heard this Jacob.

JACOB. Wrong! I have already done both.

COPELAND. Jacob, I think you should leave. I have to think about this case.

JACOB. You're not going to stay with this? Are you?

COPELAND. I don't know. But how can I just walk away now?

JACOB. Easy. Just do it. You don't want to get involved with this. If the police found drugs on them, what can you do?

COPELAND. Did the police have the right to stop, then search them?

JACOB. Come on, you know there's plenty of drugs in those projects. Now they might be in the collective.

COPELAND. Wait! Wait! Jacob. You are going too far.

JACOB. We been doing just fine for seven years without these kinds of problems. We don't need them. Suppose the press picks up the story. Our group is beginning to represent something in this city. I won't let it go down the drain over a guy who might be a real loser!

COPELAND. You being very selfish and narrow minded.

JACOB. You got to drop this case. Get someone else in your office to handle it. Look, Copeland. (*He moves closer to her*) Let's not waste our time on this anymore. We got more important things to think about. Like, your show on Newbury Street.

COPELAND. I haven't forgotten about the show. He needed me. Johnnie is a very proud young man. In some ways he reminds me of my father. He grew up in the projects in Philadelphia. He became a doctor because a social worker took an interest in him, helped him get into a summer enrichment program. And now Doris has come by.

JACOB. When it rains, it pours. I don't see how you can keep up with all this.

COPELAND. Do I have a choice?

JACOB. You have plenty of choices. You've done well in corporate law. You can do the same in painting. With your talent you can exhibit maybe in New York's Soho District. That is your future, not the criminal courts of Boston.

COPELAND. Jacob. I need to help Johnnie get out of jail. You should have seen his mother, Emma, in court. I'm worried about her. The judge set bail at $4,000. They can't raise the money. Can you help them? Put up the bail?

JACOB. (*Moving toward her*) No. I can't.

COPELAND. Why not. You got the money. It's not going to do any good sitting in the bank. And you'll get it back at the end of the trial.

JACOB. If he doesn't skip town.

COPELAND. Then leave.

JACOB. O.K. I will put up $2,000, for you. Just for you. He has to come up with the rest.

COPELAND. Why do you have to be so tight? What's $4,000 to you?

JACOB. It's my money.

COPELAND. When can I get the $2,000?

JACOB. Now. (*Takes out check book, writes and hands her a check. The lights slowly fade as Jacob stares at Copeland and walks toward the door*).

END OF ACT I

ACT II
Scene I

The scene opens in Emma's apartment with Johnnie dancing around to rap music. Suddenly there is a knock at the door. He goes and opens the door and Copeland enters.

COPELAND. Hi. I was to meet your mother here to talk about your bail, but I see you're out.

JOHNNIE. No thanks to you.

COPELAND. I gave it my best.

JOHNNIE. Yeah, but your best wasn't good enough. I thought you could do something for me. You being a sister and all. And a big downtown lawyer.

COPELAND. You raised the bail money?

JOHNNIE. What is it to you? You didn't give me the money.

COPELAND. I couldn't use my personal money. It wouldn't be right or ethical. But Jacob did give me a check for you. $2,000.

JOHNNIE. Who's talking about right? It wasn't right for those rollers to kick my ass was it? It wasn't right for that faggot judge to deny me the freedom of the streets, was it? And as for Jacob's money, you keep it. Buy yourself a red sweater or a pretty blue fall hat. I owe too many people already.

COPELAND. Well, it's here if you need it. (*Puts check on table*) But I have to talk with you.

JOHNNIE. About what?

COPELAND. About the case.

JOHNNIE. I don't want to talk to you. I want to get a paid lawyer. This here ain't gonna work.

COPELAND. What do you mean a paid lawyer. I'm not a free lawyer. My firm has given me permission to take this case *pro bono*. I had to beg to get it. They will stand behind me.

Robert Johnson, Jr.   39

JOHNNIE. Pro bono? You just like a public defender? Lady, I ain't gonna wind up like half the dudes around here, in and out of Charles Street Jail, then Walpole Prison. No, not me.

COPELAND. I'm not a public defender.

JOHNNIE. Those 5.0 bastards beat me right out there in front of the old store and then again when they got me to the station. I'm not going to be a punching bag for no body.

COPELAND. I'm sorry about that. I really am. They shouldn't have beat you.

JOHNNIE. They beat us all the time. If you wrote a book about all the brothers around here beat up by cops for no reason other than being black, you would have a book of stories long enough to stretch from here to the moon. And you know how far the moon is from here?

COPELAND. I'm not saying the police don't beat black men.

JOHNNIE. You see this system can tolerate black women. But they have no use for us, unless we playing sports or singing and dancing.

COPELAND. It's not exactly easy for me either.

JOHNNIE. What you talking about, sis. You living out there in the suburbs. You a big downtown lawyer. You got it made.

COPELAND. I still face prejudice every day.

JOHNNIE. Who you bull shitting?

COPELAND. It doesn't matter what kind of degrees you have, I always feel as though I'm on display.

JOHNNIE. Well, I'm a dead display unless I get that bail money back.

COPELAND. You get it back when you show up for trial.

JOHNNIE. But I need it in two weeks. I got to get it back to the people.

COPELAND. What people?

JOHNNIE. My crew. Can we get to trial in two weeks?

COPELAND. No.

JOHNNIE. Why not, I got to have this money lady. People don't let you just have money around here. When they say you got to have it back, you got to have it back. Why can't you get this thing taken care of in two weeks?

COPELAND. Well, first I have to get motions filed, then there has to be hearings on the motions, then the court will set a trial date.

JOHNNIE. Then get another judge!

COPELAND. Can't do that. There has to be grounds.

JOHNNIE. I got plenty of grounds, the man was prejudiced.

COPELAND. Prejudiced? I can't prove that. He's black

JOHNNIE. The only thing black about him was his robe. We use to be lynched by folk in white robes, now they're black.

COPELAND. He just didn't see the facts our way.

JOHNNIE. Then he's prejudiced. If he wasn't, he'd see it our way.

COPELAND. Listen Johnnie, I'm gonna go. I will not stand here and debate you. *(Starts to leave).*

JOHNNIE. Hold on, don't get so uptight.

COPELAND. I got a lot of work to do on this case.

JOHNNIE. Then lighten up. I'm the one who should be uptight.

COPELAND. What the police did to you was wrong. If we don't get prepared for that trial, that judge will send you away for a long time.

JOHNNIE. Even though I'm innocent?

COPELAND. Yes, but the jury will have to find you guilty first.

JOHNNIE. Will there be any blacks on that jury? Any young people from these here projects? The dudes around here know me. They know I don't do no drugs and I don't sell it. Put them on the jury, they'll find me not guilty. They'll find those cops guilty. That's justice. Real justice, not that circus they got going on downtown. And how come everyone down there locked up is black?

COPELAND. I don't like that either. It's unfair! You and me know, black are not the only ones committing crimes. But the chances are you will have diversity on the jury.

JOHNNIE. You from around here?

COPELAND. No. I live in Brookline.

JOHNNIE. Did you grow up there?

COPELAND. No. Why all these questions? *(She stands).*

JOHNNIE. Because I want to get to know you. You want me to put my life in your hands and not know nothing about you! I might be poor, but I ain't stupid.

COPELAND. I know you're not stupid. I'm here because I believe in you. Your mother was at the court and her friend Doris was there too. I promised your mother I would help you. It won't be easy. As far as the questions about where I grew up is concerned, go on and ask them if they make you feel better.(*She walks over and stops about five feet from him*). I'm looking at a young man who has a bright future ahead of him, who has been charged with a serious crime that he didn't do. I'm looking at a young man who's scared that Justice will not serve him well. Johnnie, I can't tell you that this system is fair or that it isn't racist, but as sure as I'm standing here it will determine what your future will be.

JOHNNIE. That's exactly what I'm afraid of.

COPELAND. I'm not that system that you are afraid of. I'm a young black woman who decided to take this case when others in my firm said I was crazy. I believe in you.

JOHNNIE. You do, do you?

COPELAND. O.K. The bail hearing didn't go the way we would have liked it to go, but next we have motions. I'll file a motion to dismiss.

JOHNNIE. You think you can get it dismissed?

COPELAND. It's worth a try. Sit down and tell me exactly what happened!

JOHNNIE. For what?

COPELAND. Did you have any drugs on you?

JOHNNIE. No.

COPELAND. What about the others? Did they have drugs on them?

JOHNNIE. I don't know.

COPELAND. Do they use drugs?

JOHNNIE. Ask them. I ain't no snitch.

COPELAND. I'm not asking you to tell on anyone. I'm just trying to get your defense together.

JOHNNIE. My defense is that I didn't do it. I didn't do it. (*Raising his voice*).

COPELAND. What about Darrell and Mike?

JOHNNIE. I'm not saying Jack squat! Nada! Nothing. I have to live around here lady. No. I will say nothing about those guys. I don't know nothing about no drugs. Period.

COPELAND. If we can show that they had the drugs and you had nothing to do with it because you didn't know.

JOHNNIE. No! No! You got to go at this another way.

COPELAND. What other way? You're innocent and you shouldn't carry the load for the others.

JOHNNIE. Maybe the cops planted the drugs. Like they planted that lie on Willie Bennett. We all know the Boston Police lie.

COPELAND. We can't prove that. Where's the evidence?

JOHNNIE. Where was the evidence on Willie Bennett, the brother from another project who was accused of killing a pregnant white woman, when her husband, Charles Stuart, killed her? The only evidence on him was that he was black. And being black in Boston is enough these days to get you lynched, legally. Did any white heads roll because an innocent man was ready to be sent to life in the penitentiary because a white man lied on him? Listen, if you gonna defend me and win, you got to understand how this system works! I have no faith in it. My mother has given me all that she can. She has given me encouragement and plenty of love, and let me tell you, if it wasn't for my mother, I would have done all of those things that lying cop said I did.

COPELAND. I believe you. I'll work on the motions to dismiss.

JOHNNIE. Work fast. I only have two weeks to get that money back to the people.

COPELAND. Look Johnnie. I'm doing the best I can. I'm gonna go now. I'll talk to you later in the week. (*She walks over to Johnnie and reaches to embrace him. He backs up. She exits. Johnnie puts on John Coltrane. Emma walks in*).

EMMA. Johnnie. Are you O.K.? Did they hurt you? You don't look good! (*She hugs him*) I'm glad to see you. Who put up the bail?

JOHNNIE. Friends. I got to have it back to them in two weeks. I got two weeks mother, you understand what I'm saying. The lawyer told me that we won't be through trial in two weeks. They only release the bail money when the trial is over.

EMMA. (*Embracing her son*) Don't worry son.

JOHNNIE. I don't know, ma. Laying on that hard bed in jail, I had my doubts. I knew you didn't have four thousand dollars. I was glad to see you and Doris at the court, but..

EMMA. But what son?

JOHNNIE. I don't know if we're big enough, powerful enough to beat the state. The state is bringing these false charges against me, mother. Look at this complaint, Commonwealth of Massachusetts versus Johnnie Peterson. It's not just these city cops, it's much bigger.

EMMA. Listen honey. I don't care how big they are, they'll never crush us. We'll never let that happen.

JOHNNIE. I promised you at Dad's funeral that I would make something out of myself. When you hurt your back and we moved here, I told you I would get you out soon.

EMMA. You will. I know you will son. (*The lights fade as a song plays in the background*).

Scene II

Emma is sitting in her apartment. The stereo plays Luther Vandross as Doris knocks at the door. Emma opens it and Doris enters.

EMMA. Doris! I missed you. How you been?

DORIS. You know I couldn't stay away. Hey girl. Everytime I come, you in here all hot and bothered by Luther. You in love with the man. Now he is fine, but he could lose a little weight. I like my men tight and slender. You know what I mean. (*Emma sits back down at the table*).

EMMA. (*In a soft voice*) I need to be in love with someone.

DORIS. Where's the breakfast. Where's the food child. (*Looks in the refrigerator*) Look a here, somebody been good to you. Steaks, juice and butter milk. You old home girl. Them southern roots always come out. And I bet you gonna have chitlins on Thanksgiving too.

EMMA. I don't know yet.

DORIS. Then Christmas. Everyone gets all hyped up, spending their money, running around, then after New Years everything returns to the same old boring life.

EMMA. You want it to be Christmas all year?

DORIS. Now that wouldn't be a bad idea. All year we could go around singing " Deck the halls with bows of holly" (*Singing*). Then the whole world would be broke, like me. (*Laughs*).

EMMA. You sure happy this morning.

DORIS. I guess I'm thankful. Like we suppose to be on Thanksgiving. (*Smiles*).

EMMA. But it ain't Thanksgiving.

DORIS. I know. Cut Luther down a little please. Can we do without him for just a little while.

EMMA. (*Turns down the stereo slightly*) Just for a while. (*Sits at the table*). Here have some coffee. *(She pours the coffee)* Is it cold out there?

DORIS. Not too bad. About forty.

EMMA. How's Buster?

DORIS. Don't really know. He's not at the shelter now that he got the job. I hardly see him. Did you get your phone back on?

EMMA. No, didn't get it on yet. When the last time you saw him?

DORIS. Last week. We only had fifteen minutes together.

EMMA. Why don't you go by his job at lunchtime? He takes lunch breaks don't he?

DORIS. He says he can't have visitors and all the guys eat their lunch together. He don't want to upset his boss cause it took him a long time to get the job. So he plans on working during lunch break, so his boss can see him trying hard.

EMMA. That's just like a man. When they down and out they all up in your face. But when things start going good, it's hard to find them.

DORIS. Buster ain't just no ordinary man.

EMMA. Oh Buster is special? He's different from all these clowns running around here?

Robert Johnson, Jr.

DORIS. That's exactly right. It's been rough for him. Then he got this job. I was with him, in the streets, when we collected bottles and asked for spare change. You've never had to do that. We did. Sometimes we got enough to buy hamburgers and fries. Sometimes enough for a movie just to get off the cold streets for a few hours. When the bus drops you off, you got to deal with this here world on your own. And it ain't smiling at you. Most of the people ignore you like you don't exist. They glance in your direction as they walk past you. Even if they drop a dime or quarter in your cup, they never smile, they never speak, and they never look you in the eyes.

EMMA. They probably afraid.

DORIS. Afraid of what?

EMMA. Afraid of seeing themselves in your eyes.

DORIS. People don't like to think this could happen to them.

EMMA. You know this social worker came by here this morning.

DORIS. You up on the rent ain't you?

EMMA. The hussy had the nerve to tell me that I had to put my child out in the streets or they were gonna put me out.

DORIS. What! Them people got a nerve. Like we don't even exist. What did you tell her?

EMMA. Get the hell out of my place.

DORIS. Right on sister. I wish I was here. What she look like? Some little scroungey, skinny, no-shape white woman?

EMMA. That, and ugly. (*They laugh*).

DORIS. I can believe it. (*Laughing*).

EMMA. I'm going down town to talk to the head person. She got the nerve coming here prying into my business.

DORIS. For real home girl!

EMMA. Yeah. She better hear me or I'm gonna turn the place out. That boy is my flesh and blood.

DORIS. Let me know when you go. I'll go with you.

EMMA. *(Changing the subject)* I didn't mean to say that about Buster. But he should be able to do something for you.

DORIS. He will. He's saving his money for our room. Then we'll get married there.

EMMA. You can have it here.

DORIS. Thanks, but he wants to have it in our own place. It'll mean more to him. He ain't had his own place for a whole year.

EMMA. Well, I want to be there.

DORIS. You will too, maid of honor. *(Smiles)*.

EMMA. You know. I never been in a wedding.

DORIS. You been waiting for this one, *(Laughs)*. It's gonna be swinging. Just a few folk. Buster don't have no people. I think he wants to invite a couple of guys from his job. I was wondering whether we could have a little wedding party here after the ceremony.

EMMA. Of course.

DORIS. And Luther would be here too. *(Laughs)* Plenty of big Luther?

EMMA. But he lives here *(Laughs)*.

DORIS. You got the big refrigerator for the beer and wine and a nice stereo. That's all we need. And you'll be here. That's important to me. O.K.?

EMMA. *(She pours more coffee)*. How is everything at the shelter?

DORIS. It's not the same without Buster. I don't like the people there. A few new faces. There's a guy who sits next to me every day on the bus. I think he likes me. Asks all these questions about Buster. Wants to know if he's in jail. I tell him none of his damn business. I just stay by myself. Don't talk to nobody, don't get involved with em.

EMMA. It must be rough.

DORIS. It gets lonely at times.

EMMA. I know what that's like, not having nobody to care about you. *(Johnnie enters)*.

JOHNNIE. Hi Ma, Doris.

EMMA. Hi, you didn't come in last night. You got that hearing tomorrow.

JOHNNIE. *(Pacing from refrigerator to stereo table)* I had things to do.

DORIS. How's the case coming?

Robert Johnson, Jr.

JOHNNIE. Why you want to know? I need money, not cheap talk.

EMMA. Wait! Who are you talking to?

JOHNNIE. I'm just tired of people.

EMMA. I understand, but this is my house. You show the house some respect. What you been doing out in them streets? You should be working with Attorney Marshall.

JOHNNIE. You think that's all I been doing. Running around in the streets. You beginning to sound like those white people downtown. Now my own mother is telling me I can't go out in my own neighborhood.

DORIS. That's not what she's saying and you know it Johnnie.

EMMA. Look, let's start all over. Let me fix you some food.

JOHNNIE. No, I'm O.K.

EMMA. You need to eat boy. Been out all night.

JOHNNIE. Alright I'll eat.(*There's a knock at the door*) Ma get that. (*He moves to the back room, and seems frightened*). If that's for me, I'm not here. (*He exits into backroom*).

EMMA. *(Opens the door)* Come on in. We were expecting you. (*Copeland enters*).

COPELAND. Hi Ms. Peterson.

EMMA. You know my friend, Doris McClellan.

COPELAND. Yes. Hi Doris..

DORIS. Well I better go. I'm gonna try see Buster over his lunch break. I tried to catch him yesterday.

EMMA. That's right. Go right in there and tell them people you want to see your Buster.

DORIS. Yeap. A woman got a right to see her man. Right Ms. Lawyer? You got a man?

COPELAND. I have friends.

DORIS. I got them too. Too many, but I'm talking about a man.

EMMA. *(Interrupting)* Well, Doris, I'll be seeing you, and have fun.*(Smiles)*.

DORIS. Bye, bye (*Exits*).

EMMA. She is so funny.

COPELAND. That she is. Is Johnnie here?

Stop and Frisk

EMMA. He's in his room. I'll get him. (*She calls*) Johnnie, Attorney Marshall is here.

JOHNNIE. (*Enters*) Hi.

COPELAND. How are you doing? Tomorrow we have the hearing and I thought I would go over everything.

JOHNNIE. I know, ma told me you were coming over. (*Johnnie turns his chair around and sits straddled*).

COPELAND. I knew you wanted to move things as quickly as possible and we were lucky to get this hearing so soon. It has been just two weeks.

JOHNNIE. I know. You don't have to tell me.

EMMA. He's been trying to raise the money.

COPELAND. How's it coming?

JOHNNIE. It's alright.

COPELAND. We may as well get started. (*She takes out a yellow pad*) I have reviewed the grand jury minutes carefully and I do not believe that there was sufficient information there to justify the indictments against you. There is no evidence that Johnnie knew or should have known that one of the other guys had drugs. I will also argue that the police procedure of stopping and frisking young Black men is unconstitutional and that the police did not have probable cause to stop you. Now if the Court agrees with me, then the charges against you will be dropped. We'll see what happens tomorrow. (*There's a knock at the door*).

JOHNNIE. Who is that? (*He stands*) Don't open ma.

EMMA. We got nothing to hide here. (*She opens the door and in walks DARRELL and MIKE*).

JOHNNIE. Heah fellas. (*He stands*)

MIKE. What's up?

DARRELL. Excuse me Ms. Peterson, but we would like to talk with Johnnie for a minute.

EMMA. He's busy talking to his lawyer right now.

DARRELL. I see, but I thought you were going to get yourself a real lawyer. (*Speaking to Johnnie*).

JOHNNIE. I decided to stay with her.

MIKE. This won't take long.

DARRELL. We'll let you get back to your lawyer. (*Smiles*).

EMMA. You will have to wait until he is finished.

JOHNNIE. Ma, this is important. It will only take a minute. (*He walks toward the door*).

DARRELL. Goodbye Ms. Peterson and Ms. Lawyer. (*The three exit*).

COPELAND. I don't think he should be with those two.

EMMA. A boy has to have friends. He cannot lock himself up in a closet.

COPELAND. I know, but we may have a shot with these motions, particularly if another Judge hears it. Otherwise, a trial might be difficult. The juries from this county are hard on drugs.

EMMA. But why my boy? Have you talked to him about what happened?

COPELAND. He told me he didn't have any drugs on him.

EMMA. Yes, he didn't have drugs and he wasn't on Massachusetts Avenue and Washington Street. He told me all about it. And I believe him. He told me...

(Lights fade to black, flashback to the stoop).

JOHNNIE (*Dancing*). Hey. I should put some of my poems to music. Become a rapper! (*Laughs*).

DARRELL. Here check this cut out man. (*He turns on the music and the three rock to the beat. Johnnie gets up and starts dancing around for about 30 seconds*).

MIKE. Look man 5.0 And them sirens again! (*Sirens can be heard in the background*).

DARRELL. Oh shit. Hope they keep moving. I don't need no trouble today.

JOHNNIE. Don't worry, we ain't doing nothing.

MIKE. When that make a difference?

DARRELL. Shit man. They getting out of the car.

JOHNNIE. Be cool man. *(Two police officers enter from stage left)*

POLICEMAN 2. Shut it off. *(Speaking to Mike)*.

MIKE. I'll turn it down.

POLICEMAN 2. You see that's the problem with listening to that stuff, it damages your ears. You see your buddy here, his ears been *(Looking at Darrell)* so damaged that he can't understand English. I said shut it off.

JOHNNIE. Cut it off Mike. We don't want no trouble.

DARRELL. We wasn't doing nothing.

POLICEMAN 2. *(Looking at Darrell)* That's the problem.

POLICEMAN. *(Looking at Johnnie and moving in his direction)* Where do I know you from?

JOHNNIE. I live across the street *(pointing)* on Adams Street.

POLICEMAN. Don't he look familiar?

POLICEMAN 2. Come here.

JOHNNIE. For what?

POLICEMAN 2. *(To Johnnie)* Let me see some identification.

JOHNNIE. I don't have none.

POLICEMAN 2. Let me see a drivers license.

JOHNNIE. I don't drive.

POLICEMAN 2. Give me a picture I.D.

JOHNNIE. *(Following Darrell)* I don't have that either.

POLICEMAN 2. What you got in that bag?

JOHNNIE. Personal things.

POLICEMAN 2. Open it up.

JOHNNIE. Why? We ain't done nothing.

POLICEMAN. That's the problem.. This is all you people got time to do. Sit on steps?

MIKE. What's this you people stuff?

POLICEMAN 2. Stay out of it. It's none of your business.

JOHNNIE. Look, I live across the street at 8 Adams Street. *(He starts to leave)*.

POLICEMAN *(Grabs his arm)*. I didn't say you could leave.

JOHNNIE. Let's go guys. *(Snatches his arm away from officer)* We don't have to go through this shit. *(Starts to pick up bag).*

POLICEMAN. Don't touch that bag. *(Policeman puts hand on gun).*

DARRELL. Watch it Johnnie! *(Johnnie stops and looks at Policeman)*

POLICEMAN. Give me the bag.

JOHNNIE. For what? This ain't Soweto. *(Johnnie picks up bag).*

POLICEMAN. Get up against the wall. (*He grabs Johnnie and throws him against the wall, searches him, unbuckling his belt, causing his pants to drop*).

MIKE. Get your hands off him! We ain't done nothing! (*The Policeman takes out a stick and hits Mike over the head. Darrell rushes the Policeman. Loud voices can be heard as sirens intensify and the lights slowly fade.*)

(*Lights back up on Emma's apartment with Emma near tears, sitting and Copeland standing over her.*)

EMMA. That's what they did to my boy. I don't care who you are. You don't treat people that way. These boys got to live somewhere. They didn't have to do that to Johnnie. No, not to my child.

COPELAND. We must let him know that we believe him..

EMMA. He already know that. Right now, he got two things on his mind, that trial and the money he owe.

COPELAND. I'm afraid those other two will get him into deeper trouble.

EMMA. I'm gonna go find my child. *(Gets up).*

COPELAND. No! You stay here *(Pushing her back into the chair)* You don't know the streets and neither do I. You've done your job. You raised him the best that you could. He'll do what's right. He's your son. (*Lights fade slowly as Luther Vandross starts to play softly*).

Scene III

The scene opens outside with the three boys in front of the stoop.

Stop and Frisk

DARRELL. Why you want to dis us like that man?

JOHNNIE. What you talking about. I didn't dis you.

MIKE. We heard you were going to rat on us tomorrow.

JOHNNIE. Where you hear that trash from, man. You know me. You guys my Crew, man.

MIKE. We heard different. Our lawyers are telling us that you gonna point the finger.

JOHNNIE. That's a lie. I wouldn't do that!

DARRELL. And what you still got that bitch lawyer for, man?

JOHNNIE. She's trying to help me. Working overtime. Who you guys got?

MIKE. Some dude from downtown. He suppose to know some people.

JOHNNIE. Know some people? Who he know?

MIKE. I didn't ask him.

DARRELL. You don't ask questions. You just lay the bread down and it happens.

MIKE. Like magic.

DARRELL. Now, word is out that that bitch of yours don't know diddley squat and she's trying to get you to punk us out.

JOHNNIE. I just told her that I didn't know nothing about drugs, which I didn't.

DARRELL. But you told her that we had something.

JOHNNIE. No I didn't. Cause I didn't know what you guys had.

DARRELL. Look man. I've got time hanging over my head. I ain't ready to go back in the joint. I ain't been out long as it is.

MIKE. And I ain't ready to visit for the first time.

DARRELL. It looks like you just out for yourself.

JOHNNIE. You wrong, man. We in this together.

DARRELL. Naw, you got that wrong. Me and Mike we gonna walk from this thing. But you, man. You got problems.

MIKE. Big problems. You owe people money and you need more money.

JOHNNIE. More money for what?

DARRELL. To get yourself a real lawyer man. That bitch might pull us down with you. We facing some big time man and if I get caught on this, they gonna surrender me on some probation bullshit and I'm away from here for at least twenty years.

MIKE. That's why you got to drop the girl and get yourself a paid lawyer.

JOHNNIE. How do I know that a paid lawyer gonna be better? How much that gonna cost?

MIKE. Our lawyers can take care of this thing. But it'll cost you five thousand dollars.

JOHNNIE. Where I get that kind of money?

DARRELL. The same place you got the four thousand.

JOHNNIE. I haven't paid that back yet?

DARRELL. Don't you think we know that. Our asses is on the line for that bread. We vouched for you, man.

MIKE. We knew you wouldn't let us down, and you would pay it back.

JOHNNIE. You mean they ain't looking for me.

DARRELL. Yeah, they still looking for you. But we worked out a plan to save all of our asses. Since you don't seem to be doing much.

JOHNNIE. You paid it?

DARRELL. Hell, no.

JOHNNIE. Been trying, but ain't been much work this summer. No busted pipes.

MIKE. But you know there's a catch.

JOHNNIE. What catch?

MIKE. You got to either pay the four thousand tonight or take more money for the new lawyer. If you take more money they'll extend the terms for two more months.

DARRELL. Give you some breathing room.

JOHNNIE. If I don't take the money?

DARRELL. You got to meet the man tomorrow.

MIKE. So what you gonna do? You gonna hang us out to dry? We stood by you, man. We didn't want to leave you locked up. So we went to bat for you.

JOHNNIE. And I appreciate it. I really do.

DARRELL. And I know what your rap is. You claim that you didn't know about the drugs. If I was in your position, I would do the same. But you think those white people downtown gonna believe you, a nigger. You guilty when you walk into that motherfucker. Only money talks. You got to have some dust to spread around. That's the way this system works.

MIKE. Tell him about Joey?

DARRELL. We talked to Joey.

JOHNNIE. I don't want to have nothing to do with Joey. He's bad news.

DARRELL. What you mean, man? Everybody around here got to deal with Joey sometime or another.

MIKE. You said you ain't got four two thousand right. How much you got then?

JOHNNIE. Seven hundred and fifty. And that's from working nonstop for the past two weeks.

DARRELL. Joey got a little trip you could make for him and he would pay you a little over six thousand cash money.

JOHNNIE. When?

DARRELL. Tonight. You got to make the delivery tonight. Then you paid up. You can pay back the bail money and still have money for the paid lawyer.

JOHNNIE. No. I can't do that.

MIKE. What choice you got.

JOHNNIE. Plenty. Thanks and no thanks fellas. I'll work this out myself.

DARRELL. You better start working overtime because this is the last inning. You dig?

JOHNNIE. Yeah, but I'm not gonna get deeper into this. There's no stopping, it seems. Now I got seven hundred and fifty dollars, which I can give up tonight. Right now.

DARRELL. That won't make it, man. You got to do more. Joey will help you out.

JOHNNIE. At what price? How much I got to give up in order to meet Joey. I got to deliver drugs to kids? Or snuff somebody out in some dark alley? That ain't me man?

MIKE. What you trying to say Johnnie? It ain't me! It ain't Darrell! You think we like having to deal with sleeze bags like Joey? Yeah, you want to go to school and read your poems to a bunch of white people? But don't you think Darrell and me want to be somebody too!

JOHNNIE. I didn't mean it like that man.

DARRELL. Them are the breaks. Sometimes you got to make hard decisions. They want their money.

MIKE. We just trying to help man. We all in the same boat. Where can we go? Tell us where we gonna get the money to beat these phoney charges? What we gonna do? Go down to the First National and get a loan? They don't deal with no niggers like us. Only bitches. All behind the counters, who they got? Bitches! They don't hire no niggers!

JOHNNIE. Why you talk like that man? You changed. Seem like you lost all respect for women, for your mother.

MIKE. (*Moving toward Johnnie*) Don't talk that shit to me man. I'll fuck you up.

DARRELL. (*Stepping in between them*) Stop the shit now! We got to stand together!

JOHNNIE. How can I stand together when I didn't do a damn thing? I don't know where the cops are coming from with the drugs on me. I don't know nothing about drugs.

DARRELL. But what matters in this country, in this white man's land, is that a white cop said you did.

JOHNNIE. That cop is lying!

MIKE. What's new?

DARRELL. They don't care about that Johnnie. All they want is another blackman's body behind bars. Yesterday they took away guys we grew up with. Today it's us. Tomorrow it's be our sons. It's our time. We got to fight.

JOHNNIE. With what?

DARRELL. Sometime with guns. Sometime with money. This time it's with money.

JOHNNIE. Which I get from Joey!

DARRELL. Right.

JOHNNIE. I have never said a word to him. You got the $4,000 for me. And is he gonna listen because I owe him money. He's already looking for me. I need some back up. Maybe you could talk to him for me. (*Looks at Darrell*).

DARRELL. You got to look out for yourself here. I spoke to him and set everything up.

JOHNNIE. I thought we're a crew.

DARRELL. We are. And like I said, sometimes we need more than money. (*He hands Johnnie a gun*).

JOHNNIE. What am I gonna do with this?

DARRELL. Protect yourself. In case I don't reach Joey before some of his boys run into you.

JOHNNIE. They looking for me?

DARRELL. Yeah.

JOHNNIE. Here. (*Hands gun to Darrell*). I don't like this.

MIKE. Johnnie, It's just for protection. Joey has already done time for murder. Take it man. I don't want to see you go down like that.

DARRELL. Be safe man.

MIKE. So what you gonna do?

JOHNNIE. I got to think on it.

MIKE. Think quick.

DARRELL. And do it tonight. You know where to reach us.

JOHNNIE. I got you. (*As he begins to walk off stage, Darrell puts the gun under his shirt*)..

DARRELL. And don't punk us man. You hear? (*Lights fade*).

JOHNNIE. I heard everything you said. I got to pay the money tomorrow or meet Joey tonight. I got you. (*Lights fade out*).

Scene IV

This scene opens at the Peterson apartment later that night. The lights are low and a slow John Coltrane piece plays as Johnnie enters the apartment. He turns up the lights and sets a knapsack down on the table. He stands and begins to speak aloud.)

JOHNNIE. People crying as hunger rocks the inners of their soul. Begging for relief from those whose hearts are cold. Lifting one's head to the omnipotent power. Hoping their agony will be graced by a tropical shower. Someone once asked. What is the source of this misery so vast? No one has yet listened as time slips further into the ever-growing wilderness of the past. (*He sits back down, picks up an envelope on the table, opens it, and begins to read*).

Dear Ms. Peterson:

You are hereby notified to give up and deliver the premises occupied by you as tenant of the Boston Housing Authority because of the possession of controlled substances by your son Johnnie Peterson. You must vacate the premises immediately.

(He balls the paper up, slams it down on the table, reaches into his bag and takes out the gun, stands and heads for the door when his mother, Emma enters. The lights fade up slightly as Coltrane plays in the background)

EMMA. I thought I heard you out here.

JOHNNIE. (*He puts the gun behind his back in an attempt to hide it from his mother*) Yeah, I was just getting ready to leave.

EMMA. It's two o'clock in the morning and you going back out? You have that court hearing!

JOHNNIE. (*Cuts her off*) I know about the hearing. But I'm not ready.

EMMA. What you mean? You're ready. Ms. Marshall is ready. I'm ready.

JOHNNIE. You might be. But I'm not. (*He starts to walk past her*) You think I'm ready to walk into that courtroom and tell that Judge the cop is lying. You heard him. He said he saw me on the corner of Mass. Ave., that he was this close (*Motioning with his hands*) from me. That I punched him. You think they gonna believe me when I tell them I was in Dudley Station, buying some typing paper so that I can type some poems?

EMMA. Honestly son, I do. Because it's the truth.

JOHNNIE. Come on, get real. They gonna cook me, ma. They gonna send me away for something I didn't do.

EMMA. I won't let them do that. We'll fight.

JOHNNIE. How can we fight, when they're already pulling the rug from under us. I saw that letter on the table (*Pointing to table*). It's not fair! You didn't do nothing wrong. They gonna put you on the streets. And for what?

EMMA. They just trying to scare us.

JOHNNIE. No. They trying to kill us. They trying to pound us into the dirt.

EMMA. They can't do that.

JOHNNIE. Not without a fight. (*He raises the gun*).

EMMA. Johnnie, where are you going with that gun?

JOHNNIE. You wouldn't understand. It's a man's thang.

EMMA. (*She grabs him*) And that makes you a man? Look at all the kids running around this city with guns! Are they men? You want to be a man? Then let's see if you can walk past me with that thing in your hand and make it out the door (*Pointing*).

JOHNNIE. Don't get in my way, ma. I'm warning you.

EMMA. And I'm warning you. The only way you gonna get past me with that thing is you gonna have to use it on me.

JOHNNIE. Please ma don't make me do something that I don't want to do. I have no choice!

EMMA. But I thought you wanted to be a man? Men make choices! They can choose to live!

JOHNNIE. You don't understand?

EMMA. Why? Because I'm a woman. Boy, I been you mama, your daddy, grand daddy, your everything. And I understand more than you will ever know. I know my son. And I know that gun is not apart of Johnnie Peterson. I'm gonna take that thing. (*She walks slowly toward him, takes the gun from his hand and lays it on the kitchen table. He walks away from her*). That thing ain't the solution. You kill another person and you kill yourself. (*Emma puts gun to Johnnie's head*) Because your life will be over. Ask those hundreds of boys in Walpole Prison if their lives ain't over. Pull that trigger and you can give up your dreams of being a poet and a plumber, because when you pull that trigger you are giving up on life. And we ain't never been a quitting family. When I got disabled, I didn't quit. When I lost your father, I didn't quit. I won't let you quit. No child of mine is going to quit.

JOHNNIE. I'm not a quitter, ma. I only had that *(Pointing to gun)* for protection. I know about jail. I hear stories everyday from my friends out in the streets who been to Walpole, Charles Street and that new joint down near City Hospital. I'm not looking for trouble. But I got to get some money together. I can't think about plumbing school right now. Do you understand that. These streets are dangerous. Nobody is playing or smiling anymore. Everyone is afraid and they're carrying. If I don't beat this thing, being a poet is nothing but a dream. Now I've tried to make you proud of me.

EMMA. You have made me proud son. I'm proud that you want to make something out of your life. And the poems, they're good. I was glad you started to write.

JOHNNIE. You are. You never said that before.

EMMA. I know. I never talked about it. I thought it was between you and your father.

JOHNNIE. What was?

EMMA. Writing. You started to write the day I told you about his death.

JOHNNIE. His murder! (*Loudly*).

EMMA. Yes, his murder. I know you loved your father. He loved you. He always bragged about his only child. He was proud.

JOHNNIE. I still love him. The poems help me. They help me go on.

EMMA. Then just keep writing.

JOHNNIE. Yeah. I will.

EMMA. You keep trying.

JOHNNIE. I've tried. But maybe Darrell is right, the system only responds to money.

EMMA. You will win this case. Ms. Marshall been working overtime. You saw how she's over here all the time. She wants to see you beat this thing. She told me they got scholarship money for school and there's some people to work with you. You are a good poet son. Anyway, truth will win out in the end. It always will.

JOHNNIE. There you go again talking about truth. The only truth I understand is what I see around me. This (*Waving his hands around the room*) Orchard Park Projects! When I go out those doors everyday I see the truth.

EMMA. I have faith that things will work out. You will get the money to pay them back. It will come to you.

JOHNNIE. No. I will get it. (*He rushes over grabs the gun and leaves the apartment*).

EMMA. (*Screams*) No, Johnnie, not that. (*Coltrane plays as the lights fade*).

Scene V

This *scene opens the next day at about 4:30p.m. Copeland, Emma and Doris are seated at the kitchen table drinking Coffee. Emma is dressed in a nice dress, Copeland has a suit on and Doris has on an old but clean dress.*

EMMA. Even though he didn't come in last night, I was sure he would show up for court.

DORIS. I bet those other two know where he's at. They made me so sick, standing up there with their lawyers like they the best kids on the block. Who were those two lawyers anyway?

COPELAND. All I know is that they are very expensive?

DORIS. They any good?

COPELAND. I wouldn't say good, but slick.

DORIS. They know how to grease the right palms.

COPELAND. I don't know about that.

DORIS. I bet Darrell and Mike know where Johnnie is. Couldn't you make them tell the judge where he is?

COPELAND. No. There wasn't anything I could do, but ask for more time.

DORIS. I was surprised that Darrell pled guilty.

COPELAND. If he went to trial and was found guilty, he would be facing a surrender hearing on his probation charge which would have meant a twenty year sentence, in addition to time for these new charges.

DORIS. They call it plea bargaining.

EMMA. But if they didn't do it, why they plea guilty?

COPELAND. It happens all the time. Sometimes it's best to take sure time, rather than risk getting more if found guilty.

DORIS. I wouldn't plea guilty to something I didn't do.

COPELAND. Sometimes it's the only choice, particularly if the evidence is strong for conviction.

DORIS. Why didn't Mike do the same?

COPELAND. His lawyer is probably working on a deal.

EMMA. Since Darrell said in court that Johnnie didn't know that he had drugs, won't they dismiss the charges against Johnnie?

COPELAND. Depends on what the DA wants to do. Our problem is getting Johnnie into court.

EMMA. I'm afraid something has happened to him. I didn't tell you, but last night he went out of here with a gun.

COPELAND. No. He didn't.

EMMA. I tried to stop him, but he pushed past me and ran out in the streets. He was upset cause he didn't have the money to pay some guy he borrowed the bail money from.

DORIS. Don't worry, sis. Johnnie is a smart boy. He won't do nothing stupid. You didn't raise no stupid child.

COPELAND. She's right. We can just wait. (*She pours coffee*).

DORIS. What time you got Ms. Lawyer?

COPELAND. Copeland. Please. It's about a quarter to five.

DORIS. Oh. I got to go. Listen to this. I'm meeting Buster after work at five and guess where we gonna be at seven?

EMMA. On the bus?

DORIS. Wrong. I ain't taking no more buses to Long Island Shelter.

EMMA. Why not?

DORIS. At seven, Buster and me pick up keys to our new place. It's just a room, but it's clean. Buster had to get his boss to write a letter as a reference.

COPELAND. That's wonderful. Congratulations.

DORIS. So I got to go. *(She goes over and embraces Emma).* Johnnie will be back. You know your boy. He's just taking care of some business out there.

EMMA. So I'll be seeing you.

DORIS. You strong girl. You been my strength. You got plenty more left for yourself. Honest. Thanks baby. *(She starts to exit)* Good-bye Ms. Lawyer, I mean Copeland.

COPELAND. Bye *(Doris exits)* I almost forgot. Here. *(Reaching into her* purse) Jacob wanted Johnnie to have this check for $2,000 for the balance of the bail money.

EMMA. Tell him I really appreciate his help. I'm holding it for Johnnie. He refuses to take more money from anybody.

COPELAND. Jacob said he would help again if necessary, because you and Johnnie have been through enough.

EMMA. Oh God! If Johnnie only knew.

COPELAND. I was surprised Jacob said he would not go beyond his first check.

EMMA. Did you thank him?

COPELAND. Yes I did.

EMMA. I like the way you handled yourself this morning. I'm going to look for him before it gets dark.

COPELAND. Would you like for me to go with you?

EMMA. No, this is something that a mother must do. Go out and bring her child, out of the streets.

COPELAND. Have you heard anything else from the housing authority?
EMMA. No.
COPELAND. Keep me informed.
EMMA. You've done enough already.
COPELAND. No. I haven't. You are worth every bit of my time and effort.
EMMA. I figure I would fight em. But I ain't no lawyer.
COPELAND. I respect your courage to stand up. That's something that we women learn to do. It seems, everyday. Your strength helps me too. When I see what you have to struggle with daily, I realize that I have no reason to complain.
EMMA. Thanks.
COPELAND. Then you'll let me know when you find him?
EMMA. Yes I will.
COPELAND. So. I'll see you. *(She starts to exit)*.
EMMA. You take care of yourself.
COPELAND. I will. *(She exits. Emma gets her sweater, then leaves the apartment)*.

Scene VI

The scene opens at Emma's apartment. She is sitting at her kitchen table with her bathrobe on. It is about eleven p.m. Johnnie enters from the bathroom.

EMMA. You ready to talk about what you did with that gun?
JOHNNIE. You don't have to worry about that.
EMMA. What were you doing with that thing, son?
JOHNNIE. I was just holding it for somebody.
EMMA. You didn't shoot nobody?
JOHNNIE. Of course, not.
EMMA. What did you do with it? I won't have no guns in this

house.

JOHNNIE. I threw it away.

EMMA. Where?

JOHNNIE. In the Charles River.

EMMA. Charles River? What you doing down there?

JOHNNIE. When I left today, I had to get out of here. So I walked.

EMMA. I was looking for you. I went all over this place. All of the people you grew up with. The playground. Woodrow Wilson Court. Adams Street.

JOHNNIE. I left this place. I had to get away. See something different. So I walked to Dudley. Looked in a few stores. Then walked up New Dudley, past Madison Park High School. I walked down Newbury Street. I was the only person, it seemed, on the whole street. Down there its like black people don't even live or exist in this city. You ever go there, Ma?

EMMA. No. I haven't been there.

JOHNNIE. Well it's full of people with expensive leather jackets and women in tight skirts with their little dogs on leases. Little dogs the size of cats. People seem to be going somewhere. To do something, to meet somebody. To sit in one of those out door cafes or one of those glass enclosed ones. You know, mother, I stood there on the corner of Exeter Street. I stood there for a half an hour with my left hand in my pocket, resting on that gun. I thought as I stood there and watched the people go by, ignoring me. You know as I stood there and was ignored, something inside said, " Pop one of them motherfuckers! Make them look at me and see me for a change." My hand gripped the gun tighter and I started shifting from foot to foot. Then I thought of you. I looked around that street and I didn't see a damn thing that looked like me. So I started to walk toward Commonwealth Ave. and I kept walking until I came to the river. I sat on the bank and started to cry. When I looked in the water, instead of seeing me, I saw you, smiling. I could hear you telling me to get up and go to school. I could see you giving me your last few dollars so that I could have a hot lunch. I heard you calling me in a very gentle voice, telling me that everything would be alright.

EMMA. It will be alright, Johnnie. I'm glad you came home.

JOHNNIE. So I took my hand out of my pocket and slid the gun into the water. As it slid out of sight I heard your voice again telling me that we are not quitters. So I walked back home to tell you that I heard your song.

EMMA. (*She grabs Johnnie and hugs him*) Thanks for hearing, son. Our love will see us through whatever is ahead. We are already beginning to win. Yesterday, Darrell told the Judge that you knew nothing about the drugs.

JOHNNIE. I know. I saw Mike tonight. He told me what happened. He didn't know about the drugs either.

EMMA. Attorney Marshall got the judge to let you come in tomorrow. We can get it squared away then.

JOHNNIE. O.K. I'm ready. When this is over, you and me are going to look at that apartment in the South End.

EMMA. No. I got some people I got to talk to about this place. Somebody got some explaining to do to me.

JOHNNIE. After court, let's talk to some people in City Hall.

EMMA. As long as we finish by one o'clock.

JOHNNIE. Why? What's Happening?

EMMA. Doris is taking me to lunch and guess who I'm gonna meet?

JOHNNIE. Buster!

EMMA. Right!

JOHNNIE. Then you better get to sleep. We got a full day tomorrow and while you're meeting Buster, I'm gonna check on that apartment.

EMMA. I think I will. (*She gets up and leaves).*

JOHNNIE. Good night. And thanks.

END OF PLAY

The Train Ride
(New York City, 2001)

Author's Note

This play is based, in part, upon the life of Frank Bispham. Bispham has been described as the Dean of Minority Business Enterprise in New England. From 1971 to 1974, he served as the Executive Director of the National Business League and in 1975 became Regional Vice-President. Born to Barbadian parents and raised in Cambridge, Massachusetts, he is currently the Chairman of the Citizen's Advisory Committee for the Re-Development of the growth of the former Boston State Hospital in Mattapan. The present author sits on the same committee with him and first learnt of his "Jarring Journey" as a marine during world war II at a CAC meeting on Blue Hill Avenue, Mattapan. The play focuses on a series of intellectually, psychologically and spiritually transformational encounters with racist bigotry in the course of a train ride with other recruits, from Boston through New York City and especially at the Mason-Dixon Line in Virginia, to the Boot Camp in North Carolina. Bispham, who later served in the South Pacific, is married to Annie Larkins of West Palm Beach, Florida, and is the father of three adult daughters and an adult son.

Robert Johnson, Jr.

The Author, Robert Johnson, Jr. (rear) with Frank Bispham (front), on whose experiences during World War II the play, *The Train Ride* is based. The play premiered in workshop at the American Theatre of Actors, 314 West 54th Street, New York City, on February 7, 2001. Photo by courtesy of Tom Herde and *The Boston Globe*.

Characters

FRANK BISPHAM, *19, A Black Recruit going to join the Marines.*

MICHAEL COOPER, *19, White Male, Frank's Fellow Recruit.*

SCOTT MACISAAC, *45, White Train Conductor.*

SAM, *50, Black Train Porter.*

ELIZA WATKINS, *65, A Devout Christian Black Woman.*

SADIE SIMMS, *19, Eliza's Granddaughter.*

The action of the play is set throughout on a train from Boston through New York City, Philadelphia, and Richmond, Virginia, to North Carolina, in August 1943, during World War II.

PLAYWRIGHTS' PLATFORM
1998 SUMMER FESTIVAL OF NEW PLAYS

presents a staged reading of

THE TRAIN RIDE

written by
Robert Johnson, Jr.

directed by
James A. Spruill

Facsimile of the Poster announcing the first public exposure of the script of *The Train Ride*, in Boston, Massachusetts, 1998.

The Train Ride

ACT 1

Scene 1

This play opens at about 7 a.m., August 17, 1943, on a passenger train that is close to New York City. The opening scene is in the forward car that is hot and noisy from the locomotive engine. As the play opens Eliza, an elderly woman is sitting and fanning herself while reading her Bible. Sadie, her granddaughter, is standing, getting ready to exit the car.

ELIZA. And can you bring me back some ice water? My mouth is so dry from this heat. And my corns are hurting so this morning.

SADIE. I was just there for water.(*Looking disgusted*).

ELIZA. *(She starts to get up)* Guess I'll try to get up and....

SADIE. No, mama. You sit there and rest your feet. Don't try to go walking around. *(Rolling her eyes).*

ELIZA. What would I do without you, child.

SADIE. I'm gonna get you that water now.

ELIZA. And tell them to put it in one of those large mason jars that we can with at home.

SADIE. You don't mean?

ELIZA. A jar. A big one. Can you do that for your grandmother?

SADIE. *(She walks around slowly as if thinking)* Mama, this is a train.

ELIZA. I know what it is. Looka here child, I been riding these things long before you came into this world.

SADIE. *(Walks over to Eliza slowly)* O.K. I'll ask. I just don't want to look country when I go up there.

ELIZA. *(Puts down her bible, gets up out of her seat and takes hold of Sadie by the shoulders)* What I tell you about pride? Pride will kill you.

SADIE. I just don't want to look like a ...

ELIZA. A what? *(Sadie turns and walks away from Eliza).*

SADIE. Nothing, Mama. I just want to leave.

ELIZA. What's ailing you?

SADIE. I been getting you ice water.*(Turns to face Eliza)*. That's all.

ELIZA. Now don't you raise your voice!

SADIE. I'm not raising my voice Mama.

ELIZA. Then, what you call it then?

SADIE. I'm just not sure anymore, Mama. About everything. *(Throwing up her hands)* I just wasn't prepared to find Mother in Boston the way she was. *(She embraces Eliza, who cuddles her in her arms)* And it's hard for you to get around.

ELIZA. I told you before we left that Louise was slipping.

SADIE. Slipping is one thing. But she's sick, real sick. *(She breaks away from Eliza, puts her hands behind her back and looks up, intermittently wiping tears from her eyes)* Now I got all these decisions to make.

ELIZA. Just take your time. There's no rush. Take your time.

SADIE. But in one week I got to start classes at Fisk. Mother needs me in Boston. You just about cripple.

ELIZA. Pray on it child. Ask the Lord to guide you. And as for me, the Lord will provide.

SADIE. Mama. It's seven o'clock in the morning. In less than 48 hours we'll be back in South Carolina, and I'll have to decide soon.

ELIZA. Your time is not the Lord's time. You know that song we sing back at St. Peters. He may not come when you want him, but he's what?

SADIE. Right on time. *(Eliza goes back to her seat, picks up her Bible. Sadie sits next to her)* But mother asked me to come back to Boston. I been living with you all my life. I don't know nothing about that place. And I don't even know mother. You must have known that she was going to ask me that. But you didn't tell me. *(Stands up again)*.

ELIZA. *(Standing)* You been my child since you were six year old. I raised you along with our own. Yes, I knew what Louise wanted. But I had to pray on it. And I cried. Lord knows I cried. I knew I'd be losing a child. *(Takes Sadie and turns her around so that the two are facing each other)* I prayed for the Lord to guide my tongue. He never told me

The Train Ride

what to say to you Sadie.

SADIE. Well, I didn't know what to say to her either. She knew I wanted to go to Fisk. I wrote her when I got my acceptance letter. Sent her the original and asked her to frame it.

ELIZA. Louise has worked real hard to build that beauty shop.

SADIE. I know.

ELIZA. We needed to visit your Mama. She wrote that she wanted you there.

SADIE. (*Changing tone*) I'm glad we went to Boston. I really am. You still want that ice water?

ELIZA. Yes dear. I do. (*Looking at Sadie and smiling*).

SADIE. (*Standing*) I'll get it. You want something else? Something to eat?

ELIZA. No. I got food in my basket. But, I want you to have faith in the Lord. After your father died, Louise left and made something of herself. She needs our help, right now.

SADIE. No, me Mama. She needs me.

ELIZA. And I need you to trust the Lord to give you the answers. Louise has always been a praying woman, and you got to become one too.

SADIE. No. No. I got to get ready for school. You see this book. (*Raising her voice and the book, The Souls of Black Folk*) I got to have this read before classes begin. Mother and you kept me so busy in Boston that I read one page, just one page, Mama.

ELIZA. (*Getting impatient*) Sadie, you better move on and get that water. When you come back you can get down on your knees and ask the Lord for guidance.

SADIE. In this train?

ELIZA. Why not. There's nobody here but us colored folk, and believe me, they all done had to pray at some time in their lives.

SADIE. Let me get that water. I need a glass now. (*She begins to exit, when the Conductor enters*).

SCOTT. New York City, next stop is New York City. (*He tips his hat to ELIZA*).

SADIE. I'll be back Mama. (*She exits stage right*).

SCOTT. (*Looking at Eliza*) Having a good ride Mam?

ELIZA. Everything is fine, just fine..

SCOTT. This midnight train from Boston is a big hit. You can just fall asleep and before you know it. You're at your destination. Did you sleep good last night?

ELIZA. Just fine. Thank you.

SCOTT. If you need anything just let us know. We got a lot of ice water and there's breakfast in the club car. You welcome to go there if it gets too hot up her.

ELIZA. Yes sir. I thank you very much. My granddaughter has just left to get me some water and we brought our own food in our basket.

SCOTT. Going South, I see.

ELIZA. Home to South Carolina. Just visited my daughter in Boston, who's sick.

SCOTT. Sorry to hear that. Boston, now that's a place I never cared for much. Too many Yankees, I guess. *(Laughs)* Where your daughter live?

ELIZA. Shawmut Avenue.

SCOTT. The colored section of Boston.

ELIZA. They call it the South End.

SCOTT. Like I said, if there's anything I can do to make your ride more comfortable, just let me know.

ELIZA. I sure will. *(He starts to exit, but turns around).*

SCOTT. You know, I have one daughter out of seven children. She's the youngest and she's been sick all of her seven years on this earth.

ELIZA. I'm so sorry to hear it.

SCOTT. So, I know how you feeling. She been sick long time?

ELIZA. No. Just in the last year.

SCOTT. Well, I sincerely hope she gets better.

ELIZA. Thank you very much. *(Scott exits stage left. Eliza picks up her Bible, stands, looks stage right in direction of Sadie, sits back down and begins to fan as the lights slowly fade).*

Scene II

This scene opens ten minutes later in the Club Car. Sam the porter is behind a counter setting up glasses. Frank, a Nineteen year old recruit from Cambridge, Massachusetts, proceeding to boot camp in North Carolina to join the Marines, is sitting at a table drinking a cup of tea.

SAM. We be pulling in New York City soon. *(Looking at Frank, who is engrossed in his tea)* You ever been there?

FRANK. No. Never.

SAM. Now that's another place you need to see. You heard of the Apollo?

FRANK. No. *(He gets up suddenly).* You got some music around here, don't you?

SAM. Definitely. Got to keep the customers happy.

FRANK. Let me see what you got. *(He gets up to go to the counter when Sadie enters).*

SAM. Mama wants some more ice water? She kept you busy last night.

SADIE. *(Walks past Frank and to the counter)* Yes.

SAM. How's she doing?

SADIE. Just fine, thank you. *(Sam puts the water on the counter in a plastic cup. She stares at the cup and doesn't pick it up).*

SAM. What's the matter? You see some spots or something? They just out of the same box as last night.

SADIE. You wouldn't have a large jar?

SAM. For water?

SADIE. Yes. Mama wants it in a large Mason jar. *(Sam starts to laugh).*

SAM. Mason jar? Don't that beat all.

FRANK. What's so funny about that Sam? My father, who is from Barbados, drinks ice water from large jars too.

SAM. My goodness. I guess you learn something everyday.

FRANK. *(Sam looks below the counter. Frank is looking at Sadie)*

Robert Johnson, Jr.

Hello, my name is Frank.

SADIE. Hi. I didn't want to come back here and ask for a jar.

FRANK. Don't worry about it. Where you from?

SADIE. Spartenburg, South Carolina.

FRANK. I'm going to North Carolina.

SADIE. I was just in Boston though... I might have to move...

FRANK. What's your name?

SADIE. Sadie.

FRANK. Sadie who?

SAM. Here's the jar. A friend from Georgia gave me some peaches last week. And its clean. I scrubbed it real good. *(He pours the water from the plastic to the jar)*. Give my best to Mama here?

SADIE. *(Turns away from the counter)* I will, and I'll bring your jar back.

SAM. Don't worry about that old jar. I'm sure I'll find others for our southern guests.

SADIE. We don't all drink ice water out of jars.

SAM. I know. But either way, we got cups and we got jars, big jars. *(Smiles)*.

FRANK. Why don't you sit with us a while?

SADIE. My grandma is waiting for this water.

FRANK. Give it to her, then come back. We can play some cards.

SADIE. No, thank you.

FRANK. And we got some records here. Don't we Sam? What we got there?

SAM. The Andrews Sisters. "Boogie, Woogie, Company B." Dancing music. *(Looking at Sadie)* But you don't dance, do you?

SADIE. No. Sometimes. I mean, yes.

FRANK. Let me put something on and see what you can do.*(He takes the record and puts it on. He takes Sadie's hand and she moves away)*.

SADIE. I got to go.

FRANK. How about some breakfast? *(He moves toward her and she backs up with the water is one hand)*.

SADIE. We ate.

FRANK. Sam got tea here.

The Train Ride

SADIE. *(Turns down the music)* Thanks anyway.

FRANK. You got to check in with grandma. Is that it Sadie?

SADIE. No. I don't.

FRANK. Don't want to get you in no trouble.

SADIE. I'm grown.

FRANK. Are you?

SAM. Don't mind him.*(Looking at Sadie)* He's beginning to act like a Marine. *(Looking at Frank)* Why don't you get back to your cards?

SADIE. You're in the service?

FRANK. Yeah.

SADIE. Then, I'm gone. *(She turns to leave. Michael enters, but slows down and hesitates when he sees Sadie with Frank).*

MICHAEL. Sorry I'm late for the game. But looks like you're busy.

FRANK. Yeah, I am. *(He looks at Sadie).*

MICHAEL. Excuse me. I'll come back later. *(He turns and starts to exit).*

FRANK. Sit down Mike, I want to continue last night's game.

MICHAEL. You go ahead, do what you're doing. I'll look through my induction papers.

FRANK. *(Takes her by the arm)* Can't you stay!

SADIE. See you later Frank. *(She pulls away).*

FRANK. Wait! You're a...country bumpkin.

SADIE. And you think I'm simple too.

FRANK. Of course not, you're a southern beauty. *(Frank goes back to his table with Mike. Sam goes off stage).*

SADIE. You think so?

FRANK. Yeah, I do.

SADIE. Good-bye. *(She exits).*

MICHAEL. I didn't mean to interrupt anything.

FRANK. I just met her.

MICHAEL. You work fast.

FRANK. Like a jack rabbit. Ever seen one of them?

MICHAEL. No.

FRANK. Me neither. I should go find her. We can play cards later. *(Starts to leave).*

MICHAEL. I'm real sorry if I....

FRANK. *(Stops)* It's no problem. She was getting ready to leave anyway.

MICHAEL. She seemed nice.

FRANK. Yeah. I meant what I said about her being a southern beauty. (*Changing the subject. Frank sits*) Did my snoring keep you awake?

MICHAEL. No. I was out like a log.

FRANK. *(Stands and goes to counter)* Where you say you from?

MICHAEL. I told you Beacon Hill. And you're from Cambridge.

FRANK. Wow! She's tough!

MICHAEL. Kind a shy to me.

FRANK. No. I just need to impress her a little more. You know girls like to be impressed.

MICHAEL. Too bad we don't have the uniforms yet. I heard women love the Marine uniforms.

FRANK. Heah, if I show her my newspaper, that'll do it.

MICHAEL. What newspaper?

FRANK. *The Boston Globe* with the story on me.

MICHAEL. You some kind of celebrity or something?

FRANK. The first colored man from Cambridge to be accepted into the Marines.

MICHAEL. A man making history.

FRANK. My picture's on the front page.

MICHAEL. That'll impress her.

FRANK. Wait a minute. I'll get the paper and something else. *(Frank Exits. Michael walks around looking at record player and records. Sadie re-enters).*

SADIE. (*Meets Mike at counter. She walks slowly*). The porter hasn't come back?

MICHAEL. No. Not yet.

SADIE. Where's your friend?

MICHAEL. Oh he went back to our seats to get something.

SADIE. You're sitting together?

MICHAEL. Yeah. He's across the isle from me.

SADIE. I wanted to show him something.

MICHAEL. He'll be right back.

SADIE. But, I don't know if I should stay.

MICHAEL. You can leave it with me. What is it anyway?

SADIE. I wanted him to see this book. I was suppose to read it over the summer, but haven't had much free time. I was working in grandma's restaurant, then we went to Boston.

MICHAEL. I know that book. (*He takes it and looks at it closely*).

SADIE. I guess I better go back. (*She begins to exit*)

MICHAEL. I'll tell FRANK you came by.

SADIE. Is he really a Marine?.

MICHAEL. *(Walking toward her)* Yes. Why don't you wait. (*He pulls a chair to her*).

SADIE. *(Sits)* Just for a few minutes. *(She is looking around nervously)*.

MICHAEL. What's the matter?

SADIE. Nothing. It's just that I don't usually sit with strangers.

MICHAEL. There's nothing strange about me.

SADIE. Where you going?

MICHAEL. North Carolina. To Marine camp.

SADIE. Oh. *(She gets up abruptly)*.

MICHAEL. What's wrong?

SADIE. I'm going back to my seat.

MICHAEL. What did I say? Frank'll be back soon.

SADIE. Just tell him I wanted him to see the book.

MICHAEL. You don't have to rush away.

SADIE. O.K. I'll wait for a minute. *(She sits)*.

MICHAEL. When you get back home, you're back to work?

SADIE. No. I'll be starting college in a week. At least, I hope. At Fisk University in Nashville.

MICHAEL. Never heard of it.

SADIE. It's a colored university. It's quite good, has a good reputation. You ever been to college?

MICHAEL. Harvard.

SADIE. Never heard of that. (*They laugh*).

MICHAEL. How could that be when Du Bois, the author of your book *(He looks at the book)*, graduated from Harvard?

SADIE. No. He graduated from Fisk. When I first visited the school they told us all he has done for the colored people.

MICHAEL. And they didn't tell you that he got both his B.A. and Ph.D. from Harvard? (*Laughing*).

SADIE. I don't know about all that. I do want you to give this to Frank. Will you do that? And tell him I'm not a country bumpkin. (*She hands him the book. He puts it on the counter*). I don't even know your name.

MICHAEL. Michael. Michael Cooper. And I'll give the book to Frank. He'll be glad you came back. (*Scott enters*).

SCOTT. I see you got company Mr. Marine.

SADIE. (*Stands*) I was just....(*Points in the direction of the counter*).

SCOTT. It's alright. These Marines got to have some time with the girls before they ship off.

SADIE. I was just bringing a book. That's all. (*Showing anger, she exits*).

SCOTT. Testy little thing. I don't know why she so upset, I ain't gonna tell her Mama.

MICHAEL. (*Pointing to Counter*) She was just bringing that book for Frank.

SCOTT. You don't have to explain. You deserve whatever you can get before they ship you overseas. It'll be a long time before you see a girl again. She might be a little homely, but what do you care.

MICHAEL. That was unnecessary. You embarrassed her. And me!

SCOTT. Oh come on. Their first time out of the South and they want to see how you and me live. And gals like that they want....

MICHAEL. That's enough. That's enough. I don't want to hear anymore of your nonsense.

SCOTT. You'll change after you been in the service for a few weeks. (*He exits. Mike sits at Table. Frank reenters*).

FRANK. Look what I got.

MICHAEL. What's that?

FRANK. Brown rice and peas. Fish cakes, coconut bread. My mother made me a basket. Leftovers from my going away party

MICHAEL. Don't she know there's food on the train.

FRANK. Sure. Her fish cakes ain't nothing like the junk they got here. You want some?

MICHAEL. For breakfast? They must be a little stale?

FRANK. Man no, not fish cakes. *(He reaches into his bag and gives Michael a piece).*

MICHAEL. *(He begins to eat)* And this is made from fish?

FRANK. Yeah man.

MICHAEL. *(He hesitates for a second)* Well, it's wonderful that your folks gave you a party. *(Resumes eating).*

FRANK. What your people do for you?

MICHAEL. Nothing. This is wonderful. You have a napkin?

FRANK. Hey man, just lick your fingers. Like this. *(He licks his fingers).* But you got a new watch or something?

MICHAEL. Nothing. My father wasn't happy that I enlisted in the service. He wanted me to stay in school.

FRANK. You graduated from high school didn't you?

MICHAEL. Prep school. A private school.

FRANK. You must be rich.

MICHAEL. No, I'm not.

FRANK. So you finished high school. I mean prep school?

MICHAEL. I'm in college. At Harvard.

FRANK. But I don't get it. You at Harvard but signed up for the Marines. I can see where your father's coming from.

MICHAEL. I was tired of it. Didn't see no point in what I was learning. I was only there because my father went there and his father went there. I wanted to get as far away from it all, as I could.

FRANK. You definitely doing that. You want some more of this here? *(Goes through his bag)* There's plenty left. My mother believes in feeding. Here have another piece of fish. I love fish cakes.

MICHAEL. Thanks.

FRANK. And here's the newspaper article. *(Hands it to Michael).* Think she'll be impressed?

MICHAEL. *(He looks at it)* I'm sure she will.

FRANK. There's something about her. But Sam made it like she's all religious and stuff. I never go to church.

MICHAEL. Don't worry about it. You'll manage fine.

FRANK. Let's get back to that card game. *(He goes through his pockets and bag)* Damn. I left them in our car. I'll be right back. *(Frank Exits. Sadie comes into view).*

SADIE. Did you give him the book?

MICHAEL. Not yet. It's over there. *(Pointing)* Look at this. *(Gives her the newspaper).*

SADIE. This is his picture.

MICHAEL. He says it's a little article. Looks big to me.

SADIE. This is really him. I'm impressed. "The first colored...."

MICHAEL. You can bring it back later.

SADIE. I will. *(She tucks it under her arm).*

MICHAEL. *(Standing)* I'm sorry about that conductor.

SADIE. It was nothing. He was just tired. That's all.

MICHAEL. You were visiting Boston?

SADIE. Visiting my mother. First time out of the South.

MICHAEL. You like it?

SADIE. It was alright. *(Smiling)* I prefer home though.

MICHAEL. Why don't you sit and wait for Frank?

SADIE. I can't. My grandma is real strict. I'm not suppose to talk to boys, strangers, and especially soldiers.

MICHAEL. What's wrong with soldiers? *(Smiles).*

SADIE. I agree. But my grandma... It was nice talking to you. *(She turns to exit).*

MICHAEL. I'll tell Frank you came by.

SADIE. Good bye Michael.

MICHAEL. Bye. *(She exits. Michael walks over to counter and picks up book. Scott enters).*

SCOTT. I got to say, you Marines are up and about at the crack of dawn.

MICHAEL. It's way past dawn.

SCOTT. I hear you from Beacon Hill.

MICHAEL. It seems like you all ears on this train.

SCOTT. It's my business son. To know everything. Especially on my shift. *(He walks over to counter and picks up book. Reads the title aloud).* The Souls of Black Folk. It looks like that colored Marine friend of yours finding out he's got a soul. *(Laughs).*

MICHAEL. The book is mine. *(He picks it up).*

SCOTT. Why you reading about colored people?

MICHAEL. Mr. Du Bois is a Harvard man. A graduate the school is quite proud of. Any other questions, Mr...

SCOTT. MacIsaac. And you?

MICHAEL. Michael Cooper.

SCOTT. Well, Mr. Cooper, I better get on with my chores. We'll be in New York City in a jiffy. So long, Mr. Cooper. *(He exits.)*.

FRANK. *(Enters)* I got to beat you at our card game. *(Sits back down on stool at counter)* You got a girl friend? *(Looking at Michael)*.

MICHAEL. No.

FRANK. What's the problem?

MICHAEL. No problem. Just haven't met anyone yet.

FRANK. Didn't you meet girls in prep school?

MICHAEL. All boys school.

FRANK. Bingo! That's the problem. And where was this school?

MICHAEL. New Hampshire.

FRANK. In the woods and no girls?

MICHAEL. We kept busy.

FRANK. I bet you did. *(Laughs)* Whose idea was that?

MICHAEL. My father sent me there for my senior year. Then I moved back home and started college.

FRANK. Any coloreds there?

MICHAEL. No. But we did have a servant. Sylvester.

FRANK. A servant?

MICHAEL. Yeah. What's wrong with that? We paid him well! My mother needed the help.

FRANK. I was talking about Harvard and then you jump to servants.

MICHAEL. Oh, I thought...You meant at home.

FRANK. Any colored students?

MICHAEL. I remember one girl from Radcliffe who was in my Russian class.

FRANK. Have you ever had any colored friends?

MICHAEL. Look Frank, the only coloreds I ever knew well were servants. Wait a minute. (Thinks) My freshmen year, there was a fella from Georgia, who was very smart and in my fencing class. I always had to fence against him. Every time I left that class, I had whelps all over my chest. I think it was his way of getting back. *(Laughs).*

FRANK. How many years you stay at Harvard?

MICHAEL. Three. I told my father I was leaving school and going into the Marines. He had a fit. He said the Marines were not dignified enough, that they were a bunch of uneducated red-necks. A prep school and Harvard man should go into the Army as an officer. So I left home. Went to Canada.

FRANK. Weren't you afraid? Being on your own?

MICHAEL. Best thing I ever did for myself.

FRANK. What was Canada like? My father was there once.

MICHAEL. I met some guys who had joined the Canadian Army. Spent a lot of time with them.

FRANK. What they like?

MICHAEL. We talked a lot about the war. We all decided that we had to stand with England and France. My family roots are in London.

FRANK. So that's why you're on this train?

MICHAEL. I'm here because I made a decision to be here. For the first time in my life I feel that I am doing something important.

FRANK. You ever fire a gun?

MICHAEL. No. You?

FRANK. Only at amusement parks.

MICHAEL. That's more than me.

FRANK. *(Changing the subject)* O.K. I got that deck of cards. You want to play *bid whist*?

MICHAEL. How about *gin rummy*?

FRANK. Whatever you say. *(Frank is reaching for a table).*

MICHAEL. We got a long ride ahead of us, Frank. And we got a lot of talking to do. *(Lights fade).*

Scene III

Lights up in Club Car. Sam, the porter is behind the bar, while Frank is sitting at counter, talking to him. It is about 1 p.m.. The train has passed through New York City and is close to Philadelphia.

SAM. Having a nice ride?
FRANK. As nice as it can be in those hard seats.
SAM. Careful! Careful! Don't talk about the real estate. (*Laughs*).
FRANK. Where you from Sam?
SAM. Here and everywhere.
FRANK. I'm from Cambridge. You know Cambridge?
SAM. Do I know Cambridge? I went out with a Harding girl.
FRANK. The second hand clothing man?
SAM. He was a businessman. He would let you put some cash down and pay the rest on a monthly installment. You take the merchandise after the down payment.
FRANK. That's the way I paid for my graduation suit. Little bit at a time. Job here and there.
SAM. A working man?
FRANK. Took after my father.
SAM. Worker huh?
FRANK. Working since he was sixteen. Left Barbados on a full mast schooner. An able bodied seaman. Then he went to work in the gold mines in South America.
SAM. We can get them kind of jobs.
FRANK. He prayed everyday that the mine didn't cave in on em. Next, he joined the British Merchant Marines. Visited Canada.
SAM. I heard it's not like here.
FRANK. Yeah. But they do stare at you. My father is coal Black. He told me when he got off the ship in one of those small Canadian towns, the kids followed him around staring and pointing. They had never seen a man as black as my father. After about an hour of that, he turned and went right back to the ship.
SAM. So you got work in your blood?
FRANK. Damn right! Did you see my picture in the paper? *(He looks around for it).*
SAM. No. But I heard about it. You ready for the South?
FRANK. What's there not to be ready for?
SAM. Plenty.

FRANK. When I get off this train, I'm ready for the South, the war, the women, everything. You hear me?

SAM. I hear you.

FRANK. How long you been working for the railroad?

SAM. Ten years.

FRANK. How's it been?

SAM. Steady pay. Steady pay.

FRANK. This will be my first job.

SAM. Ain't you scared of being shipped to Europe?

FRANK. They told us we'd probably be on some Islands. Near Hawaii.

SAM. Hey that's better than being up against them Germans. *(Pointing to his skin)* I heard they don't like this.

FRANK. I thought it was Jews they didn't like?

SAM. Listen. I done heard some stories about colored GI's in Europe. Man, in France, the women were told we had tails.

FRANK. You kidding me, Sam.

SAM. If I ain't right, I ain't colored. I know some guys who did big time in the stockade for talking to some of them girls over there.

FRANK. German jails?

SAM. No, young fella. Uncle Sam had the lock and key.

FRANK. Well, I won't have to deal with that. *(Smiling)* I'll be surrounded by nice Hoola girls.

SAM. You might get some play there now. Especially with that Marine uniform on.

FRANK. What you got to drink?

SAM. Everything you see up there. *(Pointing to a line of sodas)* It's almost one thirty. At suppertime, I bring out the tea. *(Looking at his watch).*

FRANK. Married?

SAM. Naw! I'm trying to get away from a woman.

FRANK. You running from women? I'm trying to find me a good one.

SAM. You'll be searching all your life. You hear me. A woman only wants what she can get from you. If you got it and give it to her, she'll stay around. As soon as your well runs dry, bye! You hear me, Bye!

Bye!

FRANK. I'll take *Dr. Pepper*.

SAM. You got it. (*Gets drink*). Here I'll have one with you. (*Opens another bottle*). You know I met this sweet, cute, little thing down at Molly's.

FRANK. Where's that?

SAM. Let me tell you little fella. Molly's got some of the finest young women you ever want to meet. I mean real, real fine women. Got everything up here. (*Pointing to his breast*) And here (*Pointing to his rear*) Where it really counts.

FRANK. No! (*Laughs*).

SAM. If I ain't right, I ain't colored. So anyway I met this high yella gal down at Molly's. And I was swept off my feet. A big nose job.

FRANK. Big enough to drive a truck through? (*Laughs*).

SAM. You got it young brother. I thought about this girl day and night, night and day. You understand what I'm saying?

FRANK. Yeah. I'm listening.

SAM. Every time I'd go through D.C., I'd bring her a present. Bought her stuff from Providence, Boston and New York City. To make a long story short, she asked me to marry her.

FRANK. What!

SAM. Stupid me. I said yeah. Had only known the girl for three months. But the poontang was good. You know what I mean?

FRANK. Yeah, yeah. I do.

SAM. When I had lay overs I'd stay at Molly's. It was owned by a colored fella and the only place we colored guys could stay at in D.C. Plenty of guys done messed up their marriages over Molly's.(*Scott, the conductor enters*).

SCOTT. Sam you seen my overnight bag?

SAM. You put it behind the counter. Here it is. (*He bends down and picks it up*).

SCOTT. Thanks. (*Turning to Frank*) You one of these young Marines?

FRANK. Yes sir. Frank Bispham. I'm on my way to Montford Point, North Carolina. Camp LeJeune.

SAM. I was just telling him about Molly's.

FRANK. You ever been there? *(Looking at the Conductor)*.

SCOTT. No, sonny. I haven't. *(Looking at Sam)* You checked the supplies Sam?

SAM. Yes sir.

SCOTT. We need to get more ice in Philadelphia?

SAM. No sir. We got a plenty.

SCOTT. When we pull into the station, take the cash receipts book in the office for reconciliation.

SAM. Yes sir. As always. Anything else sir?

SCOTT. No. That'll be it for now. Well, let me do my final check. We'll be pulling into Philadelphia in a little while. See you later Frank. *(He leaves)*.

FRANK. Yes sir.

SAM. So anyway I was saying. These guys had women all up and down the east coast. You know that can get expensive too. You got to have the right clothes. Usually two sets. When you leave home you got your uniform on, when you get to Molly's you got to be clean. You understand?

ELIZA *(Enters)*. Excuse me sir.

SAM. Yes, mam. What can I do for you?

ELIZA. I would like a cold drink of ice water. I sent my granddaughter up here for a snack and a large ice water.

SAM. You know these kids. They got their own minds. *(He takes out a Mason jar and shows it to her)*.

ELIZA. That'll be just fine. *(He pours the water. She takes her time and drinks it.)* And she took her time coming back Too. *(Frank looks around the room)*. Son, can I get another glass?

SAM. No problem. No problem at all. You having a good ride, mam?

ELIZA. Everything is just fine. Just fine.*(She finishes the water)* That was mighty good. It sure was.

SAM. Would you like some more? We got plenty of ice in here. That's one thing New York—New Haven Line believes in is ice water. They tell us keep the people cool.

ELIZA. Can I take some with me?

SAM. Why sure. And it won't cost you a thing. Water is free. Drink

The Train Ride

as much as you want. One of the few things they give out around here.

ELIZA. Can I take your jar?

SAM. It's yours. Here. Take it. *(Hands her the jar)*.

ELIZA. Thanks. *(Looking at Frank)* So long young man.

FRANK. So long. *(She exits)*. I didn't see her in my car. Where's she sitting?

SAM. Up front. There's seating up front too. This is a big train you know.

FRANK. So what happened to the girl you were suppose to marry at Molly's?

SAM. The fool took all my money and disappeared.

FRANK. What?

SAM. Yeah, but I ain't gonna talk about that. You want another drink?

FRANK. No. I better get back to my seat.

SAM. Hey, we'll be pulling into Philadelphia. Now there's some chippies here too.

FRANK. Can't get away from em.

SAM. I want to do right, but the women won't let me.*(Laughs)*.

FRANK *(Laughing)* That's for sure.

SCOTT. *(Entering)* Philadelphia! Philadelphia! Pennsylvania!

FRANK. See you later Sam.

SAM. Right.

SCOTT *(Takes a seat at counter)*. Pleasant enough, young man. We're seeing more and more colored boys going into the service. You know I was reading the other day about them colored Tuskegee boys.

SAM. Them pilots? What you read?

SCOTT. They flying fighter planes now. With the Army Air Corps.

SAM. Good.

SCOTT. But do they know what they doing?

SAM. My understanding is that theys qualified to fly.

SCOTT. And another thing. I was looking at *Life Magazine* today and they got a picture of a girl. Say she's a pilot. Here it is. *(Reaches behind counter)* Looks like to me she should be home cooking for a husband. Look at her. Looks right cute, ain't she?

SAM. I couldn't say, sir.

SCOTT. You know, how we gonna win this war if we sending girls and them Tuskegee boys? They got special training, I hear. Not good enough for the regular Air Corp.

SAM. I don't know, sir. I don't know.

SCOTT. Sam. We got to give people a little time to get use to things. People don't like to change over night. The colored fellas prove themselves in their units, then maybe they can be with the big fellas. Look at you. Started off handling baggage, worked your way up to porter. You wear a nice uniform. Make more tips than I do. (*Laughs*).

SAM. I do get the tips. Yes sir, I do.

SCOTT. Anyway you wouldn't want to take my job now would you, Sam? (*Laughs*).

SAM. No sir. Your job is your job. Mine is being porter and getting by on tips. Big tips. *(Smiles)*.

SCOTT *(Changing the subject)*. You think the Marines will whip the Japs in the Pacific?

SAM. Yes sir. If the Marines can't do it, no one can.

SCOTT. But you think colored Marines are qualified to fight?

SAM. Yes, I do.

SCOTT. With the white men?

SAM. They should be able to fight wherever they want.

SCOTT. You see, that's wanting too much. White soldiers can't fight where they want.

SAM. I meant to say, I hope this war is over soon.

SCOTT. It will be, when all them damn Japs are dead.

SAM. What about Hitler?

SCOTT. Forget Hitler! At least he stands up and fights you like a man. Not this cowardly stuff. Surprise attacks. Suicide flights.

SAM. Hitler fights man to man is what you say?

SCOTT. Like a fighter. Toe to toe. Face to face.

SAM. Why don't they let the colored soldiers fight in Europe? Fight Hitler. Toe to toe? Face to face?

SCOTT. And give all them colored fellas guns?

SAM. Sure. Why not?

SCOTT. You ever shoot a gun, Sam?

SAM. No.

SCOTT. That's my point.

SAM. What's your point?

SCOTT. We can't have all them boys with complicated rifles running around out there. You need to have smarts to fight a war like this.

SAM. We don't have smarts?

SCOTT. That's not what I'm saying. You twisting up my words.

SAM. Twisting! You saying that colored men ain't smart enough.

SCOTT. I'm not saying that at all. You just too touchy.

SAM. Touchy? (*Raising his voice*).

SCOTT. Who you raising your voice to?

SAM. I'm sorry sir. I truly am. I didn't mean to raise my voice. I beg your pardon sir. (*Silence*).

SCOTT. I accept your apology. We can discuss important things without you raising your voice.

SAM. You right sir. I am truly sorry.

SCOTT. And another thing. How we gonna have soldiers living together out on the field, when they don't do it at home. It would be a big inconvenience.

SAM. Yes sir. It would be.

SCOTT. Look, Sam, my job is conductor. The engineer has a job. Driving this here train. You have a job. Do you know how to drive this train?

SAM. No. I don't.

SCOTT. You do know how to do your job?

SAM. Been doing it for ten years now. And I'm a dues paying member of the Brotherhood of Sleeping Car Porters.

SCOTT. I don't want to hear nothing about your union and that Randolph fella. A lot of us think he's a communist.

SAM. A. Philip Randolph stands up for us colored porters. Now we have rights. And if you have some problems with my work, you can fill out a form, but I don't have to take no abuse. No, no more.

SCOTT. You not getting no abuse from me. Seem like the good white folks been getting abuse from Mr. Randolph and his people. You remember two years ago when he got the colored people all riled up, said he was gonna march on Washington.

SAM. President Roosevelt listened too, didn't he?

SCOTT. Your people got to go slow. Work your way up. You and me can't drive this train. We can't run no big companies. Damn, I can hardly keep all my bills straight every month. There are some things that we can't do. You and me ain't General Eisenhower or Patton. We ain't never been even private first class. I never went past the eighth grade and you probably never went much further.

SAM. I graduated. Got my diploma.

SCOTT. Well, that's good. The point I'm making is that we need to leave those big things to the President, the generals, the big people. You and me should just be glad we working on this train, right Sam?

SAM. Yes sir. Working on this train. It's better than shining shoes or running elevators in department stores.

SCOTT. If God wanted things different, he would have made them different. Isn't that right?

SAM. Yes sir. God knows what he is doing. That's why Hitler is killing up the Jewish people over there!

SCOTT. Who told you that! You got no proof that he's killing Jews! That's all propaganda!

SAM. I do read the papers that's left behind in the seats. I got a long time to read and I read them every day.

SCOTT. You know these Jews here in America want you to believe anything. You believe Germans would put people in ovens. It's propaganda! That's all it is. Christian people wouldn't do it!

SAM. I believe it. I done seen things happen here, right here in this country to colored people.

SCOTT. *(Getting angry)* You haven't seen no colored people put into ovens!

SAM. No, I haven't. But I've seen. No, I've heard about people. Colored people being lynched, hung from trees!

SCOTT. That's it. You've heard, but you haven't seen. That's called propaganda. Someone writes something and they want you and me to believe it. That's propaganda! You got to look out for propaganda! Don't believe what you can't see. You understand, Sam? The only thing written I believe is the Holy Bible!

SAM. I understand. *(Changing the subject)* We're in Philadelphia now. I need to go into the station, to the office.

SCOTT. O.K. I'll see you later. I'm sorry if I got a little hot about this war thing. We all Americans. We got to stand together. As one.

SAM. It's O.K. It's fine. See you later. *(Exits. Scott puts his hand down on the counter, drops his head, then leaves).*

Scene IV

The scene opens at about 4 a.m. in the Club Car. The train has passed through Philadelphia and is near Washington D.C. The lights are low as Sadie makes her way through the car. She stops next to Frank, who has his head on table, and touches his shoulder.

SADIE. Frank..

FRANK. *(Waking up)* Yeah. Are we there?

SADIE. It's me. I stopped in your car and didn't see you. Michael said you came back here so your snoring wouldn't bother anybody.

FRANK. Oh! *(Turning around)* What time is it?

SADIE. It's morning. We're getting close to Washington, D.C. You're the only one here?

FRANK. Sam probably somewhere around.

SADIE. Frank we've been on this train for twenty-six hours. *(Walking around, throwing up her hands as she walks).*

FRANK. And you had to take a walk?

SADIE. Yeah. I couldn't sleep. I was just thinking. Thinking all the time. We'll be in Washington, D.C. soon, so I didn't want to... to ah.

FRANK. Think all the way to Washington, D.C..

SADIE. *(Laughing)* Yeah. I guess so. I don't want to do that either.

FRANK. *(Looking around)* You mind if we talk about this later? *(Gets up to leave).*

SADIE. O.K. I just want to say this...

FRANK. I thought your grandma don't like soldiers.

SADIE. So what? I'm grown. And...

FRANK. What's bothering you?

SADIE. When I met you the other night, I knew.
FRANK. Knew what?
SADIE. That you were a nice guy. And you looked cute in the newspaper.
FRANK. You saw the paper?
SADIE. Yes I did.
FRANK. I didn't know what happened to it.
SADIE. I took it.
FRANK. When I finish boot camp. I'll be shipped out, overseas.
SADIE. You don't know that for sure.
FRANK. And you do?
SADIE. Yes. Let's write.
FRANK. I'm not going to have time to write letters.
SADIE. Why are you making this so difficult?
FRANK. You barely know me.
SADIE. I know you're the first colored Marine from Cambridge. That's where your friend Mike is from?
FRANK. He went to school there.
SADIE. I know Harvard.
FRANK. How you know that?
SADIE. He told me. *(Silence).*
FRANK. You talked to him.
SADIE. Yes.
FRANK. And he didn't tell me?
SADIE. What's there to tell?
FRANK. What else happened?
SADIE. Nothing.
FRANK. When did all this go on?
SADIE. The other night when you left him in the club car and went to get the food your mother gave you.
FRANK. And you met him then?
SADIE. I didn't meet him. I just brought a book for you.
FRANK. What book?
SADIE. A book I been reading, trying to read all summer.
FRANK. I didn't get no book and he didn't tell me nothing.
SADIE. I'm sorry about that.

FRANK *(Visibly upset. Walks around silently, then speaks)* I thought you wanted to know about me. Now you telling me all this.

SADIE. I do. Keep talking. Tell me about you. I gave you the book because I wanted you to know that I'm more than a simple country girl. I'll be the first in my family to go to college. We are both firsts. I came all the way here, looking for you because I was disappointed that you didn't say anything about the book.

FRANK. Thanks for the book.

SADIE. And I wanted to know more about you. Once we get in Washington, D.C., Mama said we won't be able to move around as much. So you better talk fast.

FRANK. You know I got drafted into the Navy.

SADIE. No.

FRANK. But when I reported, I told them I wouldn't do it. *(He stops walking)* So this big sailor gets right in my face and says to me "You ain't gonna do what, boy?" He was standing this close to me. *(Motions with his hands)*. I looked him straight in the face and said "I ain't going into the Navy. I ain't gonna be no cook." I caused such a scene they took me over to an officer. He asked me where I wanted to go and I said Marines, that I wanted to fight. He sent me home and told me to come back the next day.

SADIE. You come back the next day?

FRANK. Bright and early. So I go in this office and another asked me why I wanted to be a Marine. Now I was scared as hell. *(Frank is still standing, playacting as he talks)*. I looked him straight in the eyes and said: "Sir, the Marines are the pride of the nation and I would be honored to be one." He told me I could be one of em.

SADIE. You must a been happy?

FRANK. I went home and my folks threw a party for all my friends. So, here I am.*(Not knowing what to make of his predicament)*.

SADIE. Hey, there's the record player. Want to play our song again? *(She looks through the records and puts on Andrews Sisters' "Boogie Woogie Bugle Boy")*.

FRANK. Keep it soft. I don't want Sam to come in here.

SADIE. I thought you and him were friends. Let's dance. *(She grabs Frank and they dance)*.

FRANK, That's too loud. You gonna get us in trouble.

SADIE. Good. We need a little trouble on this train. *(They dance. Frank goes over and turns the record player down. She turns it back up and they dance wildly. He twirls her around. They laugh and dance as if to exhaustion. She sings)* The Boogie Woogie Company B. Somebody's coming. *(She cuts the music off. Sam enters and catches Frank's eye).*

SAM. *(Looking at Frank)* Hey.

FRANK. How you doing?

SAM. Fine. Just fine.

FRANK. We wake you?

SAM. Time to be at work.

SADIE. I got to get back. Hi *(Waving at Sam)* We're just listening to music.

SAM. I know what you doing.

SADIE. Talk to you later. *(Looking at Frank. Smiles and rushes off)*

FRANK. I didn't mean to be so noisy.

SAM. Sit down here. I been thinking about you. You know what you getting yourself into?

FRANK. I'm gonna fight Hitler. The madman got to be stopped.

SAM. That's good. I like that. But, I bet you never heard of the Brotherhood of Sleeping Car Porters?

FRANK. No.

SAM. But you know about Hitler?

FRANK. Everybody knows about the war. Soon I'll be fighting for my country. My people may be from Barbados, but America is now my home.

SAM. There's just one little problem.

FRANK. What's the problem?

SAM. Segregation. You ever been to Harlem?

FRANK. No. But I heard about it.

SAM. That's nothing. You got to be there. You know why Harlem's full of colored people? Because they don't want us to live with them. Our headquarters is there. Before that union, my job meant nothing. If Mr. Charley didn't like the way I smiled one morning, I could be sent home, for good.

FRANK. One day on my way back to Boston, I'll visit Harlem.

SAM. Now I got job security. Our members are strong. We can strike. I know you don't know what that means.

FRANK. You be surprised.

SAM. We walk off the job. Whose gonna clean up the bathrooms, pick up the luggage, serve the food?

FRANK. You don't clean no washrooms.

SAM. I did that years ago. Now, I got seniority. The young fellas like you, that's your job.

FRANK. That wouldn't be my job.

SAM. *(Laughs).* I heard a party up in here. *(Michael enters).*

FRANK. We just played a record. She's a good dancer.

MICHAEL. The music woke me. Sam, can I get some coffee? Real black.

FRANK. I thought there was a shortage of coffee because of the war. That's what you told me Sam.

SAM. We always keep a little stash for our special guests.

MICHAEL. No cream. I like my coffee black, real black.

FRANK. I bet you do.

MICHAEL. What's that suppose to mean?

FRANK. You hear that Sam? Mike here likes his coffee black, real black. How you like your coffee Sam?

SAM. I ain't getting into this conversation. My name is Bennett and I ain't in it! *(Laughs).*

MICHAEL. I don't know what your problem is, but I'm going back to my seat. Sam, can I get that coffee?

SAM. Here it is, real black.

FRANK. You been talking to Sadie.

MICHAEL. What's that suppose to mean?

FRANK. Just what I said?

MICHAEL. What you talking about?

FRANK. She knew you were at Harvard. I didn't tell her. So you must a been talking to her.

MICHAEL. We had a short conversation. Anyway, you don't seem to show much interest in her.

FRANK. No. So what?

MICHAEL. So why you getting so hot about a conversation?

FRANK. Because I thought I could trust you!

MICHAEL. This conversation is ridiculous. I got better things to do with my time. *(He exits).*

FRANK. Wait! I still got some things I want to talk to you about. *(Sam starts to laugh.)* And where is my book?

MICHAEL. What book?

FRANK. You know what I'm talking about!

MICHAEL. Oh, the book. You want your book. (*He walks behind counter and looks for book)* It was here. Maybe it's at my seat. I'll go get it. *(He exits).*

FRANK. I'll go with you. *(Exits).*

SAM. I can see now, you all gonna have quite a time fighting this war. *(He laughs. Lights slowly fade as Sam looks into the distance).*

Scene V

The train has left Washington, D.C. and is getting close to the station in Richmond, Virginia. It is about noon, later in the day.

SCOTT. *(Shouting)* Richmond, Virginia, our next stop. The time is twelve noon. Eastern Standard time.

FRANK. These seats are so uncomfortable.

MICHAEL. What you expect?

SCOTT. *(He walks slowly up to the two men)* Young man *(Pointing to FRANK)* May I see your ticket?

FRANK. Sure. *(He goes into his back pocket. Hands the ticket to conductor).*

SCOTT. Going to Camp LeJeune?

FRANK. Yes sir.

SCOTT. Well son, you must come with me.

FRANK. Where?

SCOTT. To the forward car. It is up there. Up front?

FRANK. Isn't the train going to North Carolina?

SCOTT. Yes it is. But you can't remain in this section.

MICHAEL. Why does he have to relocate?

SCOTT. It's the rules.

MICHAEL. What rules? What are you talking about? We been sitting here for over thirty hours and now you telling us we have to move.

SCOTT. Listen. Keep your voice down please. I'm not saying you have to move. Just that your friend has to come with me. He doesn't have to leave the train, but he must relocate.

SAM. *(Walks up)* Having a problem?

FRANK *(Walks up to Sam with a big smile)* The conductor is saying I have to go to the forward car. Tell him I been right here every since the train left Boston.

SAM. He know that. He can see it on the ticket.

FRANK. Then what's going on?

SCOTT. *(Looking at Sam)* The young man won't move to the forward car.

SAM. Here let me talk with you for a second. Let's go back to the Club Car. *(Frank leaves with Sam).*

SCOTT *(Looking at Mike)* Now he tells him about the rules of the train. But, I only do my job.

MICHAEL. What rules? I didn't see no rules when I got on. Is there something you're not telling me? Has he done something wrong?

SCOTT. Nothing like that son.

MICHAEL. What's the problem then?

SCOTT. After the train crosses the Mason-Dixon Line, we must enforce the separate seating for coloreds rule. Colored people cannot sit with or in any way socialize with white people.

MICHAEL. What! But he's a Marine. Going to fight for his country. That rule is absurd!

SCOTT. I don't make the laws.

MICHAEL. Well this is crazy!

SCOTT. Please keep your voice down.

MICHAEL. I never thought. I can't believe this. And this is 1943. I'm going to Europe to fight, isn't that right? For freedom! Tell me Mr.

conductor, isn't that right?

SCOTT. Son, I could have asked him to go to the forward car after we entered Maryland. But usually let them ride anywhere until we reach the capital. After we leave Washington, we're in Virginia. It's a different world down here.

MICHAEL. Down here is America. Isn't it?

SCOTT. Haven't you ever been to the South?

MICHAEL. No.

SCOTT. Well, this is the other America. *(Lights fade down and up on the Club Car).*

SAM. Son, I thought you knew that this train was segregated.

FRANK. Segregated? I been freely moving about. When I got on, I sat in the first seat I saw.

SAM. Right this minute you riding in Virginia. They tell me that Richmond was the capital of the Confederacy.

FRANK. You didn't tell me nothing about having to move.

SAM. You ought to know!

FRANK. I've never been out of Cambridge!

SAM. Boy, down here they don't let you and me sit with them, or eat with them, or do anything with them..

FRANK. What they afraid of. This ain't gonna rub off on them. *(Rubbing his skin).*

SAM. Who you telling. I know that. But we just doing our jobs.

FRANK. Our job! I thought you were my friend. Telling me all about Molly's. You just like him. *(Pointing in direction of the conductor).*

SAM. I'm trying to put some sense in that head of yours. That man out there got the law on his side. He can ask you to leave politely. And if you don't go voluntarily, he can crack your head.

FRANK. What about all that talk about the Brotherhood? For a minute I believed that you and that Brotherhood had changed things. It looks like all it did was put dollars in your pockets.

SAM. That conductor is enforcing United States law. What are we suppose to do? You tell me.

FRANK. What he gonna do?

SAM. You don't want me to tell you. You'll get carried out.

FRANK. The hell I will!

SAM. Up in Cambridge, you might be able to live with em and run around with em. But not here.

FRANK. (*Sitting*) They can't touch a Marine.

SAM. You are a colored Marine, not a white one. That's the big difference. You are going to LeJeune. Your friend out there is going to Paris Island. You can't even fight with him. You will get segregated training, then you'll fight in segregated units.

FRANK. Damn!

SAM. Didn't you ask questions before you signed up?

FRANK. I didn't sign up. I was drafted into the Navy.

SAM. Then you real stupid. Everybody knows that there's colored troops and white troops?

FRANK. Well, I didn't. *(Stands, angry. He starts to leave).*

SAM. Where you going?

FRANK. Back to my seat.

SAM. You can't do that.

FRANK. Watch me. *(He leaves. Sam starts to walk slowly in his direction as the lights fade). (Lights back up in the coach. Frank enters and retakes his seat, followed by Sam).*

SCOTT. O.K., son. What's it gonna be?

FRANK. I'm staying right here.

SCOTT. No, you are going where I say you belong.

FRANK. I belong here. With my friend.

MICHAEL. I have no objections to him being right here.

SCOTT. That's not the point. The law sees it different.

MICHAEL. The law is set up to protect us. (*He stands*) Isn't that right? *(Walks toward Frank).*

SCOTT. Something like that.

MICHAEL. Well, I don't need protection, not from this man. He stays.

SCOTT. I say he goes. *(He reaches for Frank's arm. Frank stands and moves away from him).*

FRANK. Get your hands off me. (*Mike stands).*

MICHAEL. You have to remove me too.

SAM. Son, if you don't go peacefully, it will only get worse.

SCOTT. You will go to jail at our next stop. I promise you that. You will never become a Marine after you get a conviction.

SAM. Listen to me, he's right. These jails in Virginia are full of us. You can do better than that. Come on with me. *(He motions for Frank to follow him).*

MICHAEL. Don't go Frank.

FRANK. *(Looking nervous)* I never been in jail before.

MICHAEL *(Stands slowly and walks over between Frank and Scott)* Stand behind me. *(Motions for him to stand behind him).*

FRANK. This is our first fight as Marines. And I think we can win this, hands down.

SCOTT. *(Reaches in and grabs Frank and pulls him. A scuffle ensues. Sam grabs the other arm of Frank. Mike is held at bay by Scott with a stiff arm).*

FRANK. O.K. O.K., I'm going. Take your hands off me.

SCOTT *(Scott releases him and reads from a piece of paper he takes out of his back pocket)* I am now giving you official notice that your aggressive actions constitutes an assault upon a federal agent. You understand? I will release you only if you agree to come peacefully.

FRANK. I'm going! Let my arm go! *(Looking at Sam).*

SCOTT. You promise no more resistance?

FRANK. I promise. *(Scott releases his arm. Sam reluctantly takes his hand away).*

SAM. This way. *(Sam takes him away. The two exit).*

SCOTT *(Turns, looks at Mike and points his finger).* You take your seat before I have you put off my train. I still might charge you with being an accessory to a crime. *(Mike stands. The lights slowly fade as Mike continues to stare at Scott).*

ACT II

Scene I

The Scene opens in the forward car several hours later. It is morning and the train has moved below the Mason-Dixon Line. The noise of the locomotive can be slightly heard. Frank is sitting in one seat by himself. Across the isle from him is Eliza, who is reading a big Black Bible, and fanning. Frank is sitting, with his head down in a solemn mood. Sadie is asleep nearby.

ELIZA. Hello again. You fell asleep when you came here. You know there's a little scripture I thought you might like.

FRANK. No, thank you Mam.

ELIZA. We all need a little encouragement sometime. That's why this is called the Good Book. It's full of encouraging words. And son, you know why these here words are encouraging? Because they are the words of God. Right out of his very mouth.

SADIE. *(Gets up and walks toward Eliza)* Mama can I borrow your toothpaste? *(Sees Frank)* What are you doing here? (*They embrace*).

ELIZA. You know him?

SADIE. Yes. No. We met.

ELIZA. Met where?

SADIE. In the other part of the train.

FRANK. When she came to get your ice water.

ELIZA. All those glasses?

FRANK. Yes.

ELIZA. Jesus!

SADIE. Mama. We met one time. Maybe two. He's famous. Picture in the paper. Going into...

FRANK. It's alright. *(Moving toward Sadie, trying to silence her)*.

SADIE. What are you doing here?

FRANK. The conductor said I had to come here because I'm colored.

SADIE. He did?

FRANK. Yeah. He said I could either sit up here or be arrested in Richmond.

SADIE. That Porter didn't tell you about the colored car? That's part of his job.

FRANK. No. He didn't. What are you doing here?

SADIE. I been here since Boston.

FRANK. It's too hot. *(He loosens his collar)*.

SADIE *(She hugs him again)* Oh. It's not that bad. Mama, this is Frank.

ELIZA. I met him already. Now child, I want you to go back to your seat.

SADIE. For what?

ELIZA. Because you know my rules.

SADIE. What rules?

ELIZA. About soldiers.

SADIE. But Frank is a friend.

ELIZA. And I'm your grandmother!

SADIE. Yeah. You are. But I don't see nothing wrong with me talking to Frank.

ELIZA. Seems like you been doing more than talking.

FRANK. I saw her in the club car. But that was it.

SADIE. Anyway, he's from Cambridge.

ELIZA. That's nice.

SADIE. I didn't have a chance to meet any young people there. You had me in the house with you the entire week.

ELIZA. I don't want to hear nothing else from you child. You gather my meaning?

SADIE. Yes, mam.

ELIZA. What you did was wrong. You know that?

SADIE. Yes, mam. I do.

ELIZA. Why don't you come over here and sit by me. (*Looking at Frank)* There's plenty of room.

FRANK. I'm fine here.

ELIZA. Let me read you a little verse. Have you ever heard the passage "Everything works out for the good for those who love the

Lord?"

FRANK. No, I haven't.

ELIZA. Eliza Watkins. Mrs. Eliza Watkins. *(Extends her hand, which Frank doesn't take).*

FRANK. Mrs. Watkins. I don't need God right now.

SADIE. He'll be alright Mama.

ELIZA. Never you mind daughter. *(Turning to Frank)* But we all need God, son. Everybody. The poor, the rich. We all got to meet our maker someday. You want the Lord to say "Welcome to the Kingdom, my good and faithful servant." You know what else he might say if you not ready.

FRANK. Never thought about it.

ELIZA. "Depart from me, ye worker of iniquity, I know you not." *(She pauses, then begins again)* Are you going to make it to heaven?

FRANK. I don't know why you talking about heaven? Anyway, I think I'm a pretty good guy. But if I had to think about it. I'd say yes.

ELIZA. *(She laughs).* Don't we all wish that. *(Pause).* My husband died in the last war. Had only been in a few days. He was a cook.

FRANK. I'm sorry to hear about that.

ELIZA. And I continue to support my family this day by cooking. If you're ever in Spartenburg ask anybody where Blessed Barbecue is located. The people come from all over to get our ribs and chicken. And the white folk they there before anybody. Red barbecue covering their jaws. We always give them extra napkins, so they can keep their faces clean. It looks right funny.

FRANK. Blessed Barbecue. That's a catchy name. *(Smiles, and almost laughs).*

ELIZA. We raised five children in the restaurant. Their father taught them all to cook. He cooked so much that he never seemed to have time to go to church, to get his soul right.

FRANK. Maybe his soul was right and you just didn't know it.

ELIZA. No son, I lived with the man. If you, young man, are going into the service, to fight this war, you need something to help you, to stay with you, to be a fence all around you. You must have your soul right with God.

FRANK. My soul is right. *(Raising his voice)* Why are we here in this hot car? You, me and the others? It's too hot in this place. There you are fanning yourself to death. Why can't we sit anywhere we want on this train?

ELIZA. What you saying boy? That's just the way it is. In Boston Louise lives in the colored section. At home we live across the tracks from the white folks. You never been to the South before? That camp they just built is for colored only.

FRANK. No one told me about the train.

ELIZA. Son, there's somethings you just know. It's like breathing. No one got to teach you to breathe.

FRANK. But I'm going to fight and defend this country. Right?

ELIZA. Frank, the Good Book says be obedient to those who have authority over you.

FRANK. That's exactly what I'm doing. I got drafted. (*He stands*). I'm obediently going into the Marines.

SADIE. I agree Mama.

ELIZA. You do. Do you?

SADIE. Yes I do. Frank and I have talked.

ELIZA. You have, have you?

SADIE. Yes. We have. I know it's my Christian duty to help mother in Boston, but I want a life too. I want to go to Fisk and I want to be able to see Frank.

ELIZA. You got plenty of time to make the decision about school. But, you know I don't allow you with soldiers.

SADIE. Mama, I have already made a decision about school. In a week, I'm leaving home for college. I'll be on my own then.

ELIZA. This young man done come into our lives for a reason.

FRANK. Well, tell me the reason cause I'm baffled.

ELIZA. You should be obedient to God. He is speaking to you right now. You can listen to his voice and your life can be beautiful or you can turn your back on him. But that's dangerous, son. Real dangerous. When he calls, you should listen.

FRANK. Listen to what? Why should I listen?

ELIZA. We all must listen. "Man who is born of a woman is of a few days and full of trouble." That's scripture, son. There is no way you can escape this world. It is evil. Satan has it under his control. Many people, colored and white. They all going to hell. You must make sure you don't go.

FRANK. I feel like I'm in hell already. *(Sits back down)*.

ELIZA. No son. This ain't hell. No! No! This is mild, very mild compared to hell. Hell is going to be hot. The scripture says there will be weeping, wailing and gnashing of teeth.

FRANK. This ain't exactly the North Pole. (*He loosens his shirt collar even more*).

ELIZA. The scripture says it's going to be seven times hotter than it ought to be. Son, you must make sure you are saved. There won't be no escaping at judgement day. It'll be too late. Why don't you come over here and sit next to me. We can read the Bible together.

FRANK. I'm comfortable in my seat.

SADIE. He is happy where he is.

ELIZA. What has got into you child?

SADIE. Nothing. Maybe we should just leave him alone.

ELIZA. I'm trying to help this young man, and you make your way to heaven.

SADIE. Mama, I graduated near the top of my class at Booker T. Washington High School. I'll do just fine.

ELIZA. No. I don't think so.

SADIE. During breaks, I'll visit mother.

ELIZA. What about the restaurant?

SADIE. Blessed Barbecue is in your capable hands. And you can hire extra help.

FRANK. Sounds like you all done solved all your problems. I still got this big problem of being here in this place.

ELIZA. Just sit here. This is where you belong. *(Motioning to Frank)* We don't need to be yelling across the isle.

FRANK *(Sits next to her)* Look Ms. Watkins. I don't understand how all of you can just sit here and take what they are doing to us on this train.

ELIZA. God is no fool. He knows what we can bear.

FRANK. I know what I can bear too. *(He stands)*. And it's too hot in here.

ELIZA. The engine is right through that door. *(Pointing)* We get all the heat. We have the best seats in the winter.

FRANK. But it's August. It's eighty-five degrees outside and one hundred in here.

ELIZA. Sit back down. *(She reaches for his arm. He sits).* Here take a fan. I got another one here. *(She reaches into her bag and takes out a folding fan).*

FRANK. *(He starts to fan himself)* It's dirty, sooty.

ELIZA. It's the coal dust. When you open the windows to get a little fresh air, the coal dust blows in with the wind.

FRANK *(Standing)* We don't have to put up with it!

ELIZA. There is nothing we can do.

FRANK. Yes there is. I'm going to go right back out there *(Pointing)* and take my seat. And if they try to stop me, they'll have a fight on their hands.

SADIE. You sure you want to do that?

FRANK. Yes, I do.

SADIE. What about jail?

FRANK. This is already jail. We're confined and I haven't committed no crime! I'm going back.

SADIE. And I'm going with you.

ELIZA. No. You're not child. I done raised you to do right!

SADIE. And I thank you. But this is the right thing for me to do! You taught me that we must fight evil with good. Mama. Frank might not be a Christian, but he is a good man.

ELIZA. The scripture says "Be ye not unequally yoked together."

SADIE. Mama, we are just friends. We are not yoked, whatever that means, and he has never uttered an un-Christian word to me.

FRANK. If she wants to go with me, it should be her choice.

ELIZA. You know, several years ago, down in Spartenburg, I knew a man named James Massengill. He had just got a job in the Sanitation Department of the city. One day he was working in the white section and had to go to the bathroom. So he went in one for whites only. Four white men beat him to death. He never should have gone in. The bathroom had a big "White men only" sign out front. And you know he could read, being a graduate of Morris Brown College.

FRANK. What was he suppose to do? Pee on himself!

ELIZA. Now you know you not suppose to be up there. (*Pointing to the "white" section of the train.*) You need to stay alive! The Massengill boy had a young wife and two children.

FRANK. At least his kids know he died fighting like a man.

ELIZA. No. They were never told how their father died.

FRANK. That's stupid!

ELIZA. That's what you call it? The boy is dead. They said the boy had never met his master.

FRANK. His Master?

ELIZA. Jesus. He never accepted Christ in the pardoning of his sins. We don't know when our last day is coming. You got to be ready. Ready when he comes. You see, son, I'm ready. I'm not going to loose my soul over this world. This is just temporary. It is not my home. This is not my home. I'm working for a better place. A place that's not built by hands. I want a place where everyday is Sunday. Where everyone has a beautiful smile. Where the sky is always blue and there are no clouds in sight. I believe there's a place where peace is everywhere. Where the lions play with the sheep. That's what I'm working for.

FRANK. Well, I want to get out of here. I'm going. *(He stands. Sadie stands too).*

ELIZA. Don't do it son. And where you going? (*Looking at Sadie*) It won't be pretty what they'll do to you.

FRANK. Look what they already doing to you!

ELIZA. No sir! No Sir! They ain't doing nothing to me. I'm living my life the way I want to. I'm making preparations for a better place. You know the Lord showed me my name is written in the Book of Life.

FRANK *(Sitting and looking at Eliza)* Why don't we walk in there and take the first seat we see in the white section. They won't manhandle you.

ELIZA. Why are you pushing this thing boy? You act like you from a different world or something. Hold Still. You always trying to go somewhere. Now look here. I don't know you from the next young man in this train. But I believe that you done come into my life for a purpose. And my granddaughter sees something in you. (*Looks at Sadie*) But I do believe that the Good Lord done put you here for me to witness to you. You need to get down on your knees.

SADIE. No, mama.

ELIZA. You need to ask the Lord to forgive you of your sins. You might not come back from that war!

FRANK. I haven't done nothing wrong!

ELIZA. You were born in sin.

FRANK. No. I was born colored, that's my problem, right?

ELIZA. And you let it take your joy? Like a thief in the night?

FRANK. All I want is to be just me, not Frank the colored boy. Not the coon, the nigger, just me. I want people to see the real me, not just this skin color.

SADIE. I agree. Mama I love you and all. But I need more than helping out in the restaurant and going to church. Frank needs our help now!

ELIZA. Hush child!

SADIE. You've made me feel like I have to spend all my life repenting.

ELIZA. We have all come short of the glory of God.

SADIE. So what! Look at me Mama! Do I look like sin to you? *(Starts crying)*.

ELIZA. *(Approaches Sadie to console her)* Sadie. Sometimes love comes in forms we don't expect. But it stirs something deep down inside our hearts, and it lets us know, beyond a shadow of a doubt, that God is there. Then you know as sure as fire is hot and the water is wet, that you're doing what's right.

SADIE. Mama this train ride has opened up the world to me. I've grown.

FRANK. My father told me that in Barbados the coloreds stood together. I was born an American. That means a lot to me. Americans are going to fight and win this war. This train is full of GI's. All Americans. As I look around here I see other colored soldiers. Going to fight for their country.

ELIZA. And they not trying to be where they ain't wanted.

FRANK. But in Barbados, we stood tall. *(He sits in a seat and Sadie slowly sits as the lights fade)*.

ELIZA. This ain't Barbados, son.

Scene II

The scene opens with Frank sitting next to Sadie. The train has traveled deeper into the South. Eight hours have elapsed since the last scene. It is about 10 p.m. Eliza is sitting by herself. Mike enters.

MICHAEL. *(Tips his hat to Eliza)* Howde mam. Just seeing how everyone is doing..

ELIZA. We doing fine. But you shouldn't be here.

MICHAEL. I didn't know what they did to you. *(Looking at Frank)*

FRANK. *(Stands and shakes Mike's hand)* Not much they could do. I been here eight hours and nothing.

MICHAEL. You took a big stand. People been talking about you.

FRANK. It was nothing.

MICHAEL. All the GI's heard about what happened. We got together and decided that we would stand with you.

FRANK. That's not necessary. I been thinking about what happened. It is the law. So maybe I'll just stay here.

MICHAEL. But you not listening to me, Frank.. They can't arrest the entire car.

ELIZA. *(Interrupting)* Whatever he did, he didn't mean no harm. And you better keep it down before they find you here.

MICHAEL. None of us knew there was a colored section.

FRANK. Now I know. Anyway, we almost to North Carolina. *(Standing up)* Like I said, I will just stay put.

SADIE. I'm going to a colored college. Just like I went to a colored high school.

MICHAEL. That's not what I meant!

FRANK. *(Confronting Mike)* Mike, you don't know me, so please, don't speak about what you don't know. And I don't appreciate what you said to Sadie. Not now. Not then. Leave me alone. Go back to where you come from. And all your private schools in the woods.

MICHAEL. I thought we had come further than that. I thought we were friends.

Robert Johnson, Jr.

ELIZA. Listen boys. I think we need to change this talk. All of you is acting ugly, and yelling in this car.

MICHAEL. I'm not yelling.

ELIZA. You heard Frank tell you he's staying right here.

SADIE. Mama, you don't need to explain anything to him.

FRANK. *(Moving toward Mike)* I've had enough!

ELIZA. *(Stepping in front of Frank)* Sit down, son! We don't want the authorities to come here.

SADIE. *(To Mike)* You got to go, to leave before all of us get into trouble.

ELIZA. (*Looking at Sadie*) That's enough!

MICHAEL. You're going to give in without a fight?

FRANK. I've been here eight hours and in that time I've been thinking.

MICHAEL. I thought you were stronger than this.

FRANK. No. I mean.

MICHAEL. You mean what?

SADIE. Leave him alone Mike..

MICHAEL. I'm just trying to help him.

SADIE. No. You just trying to get him into deeper trouble. You see where he is. He is right here with us, me, my grandma and the others.

MICHAEL. But he belongs with the other servicemen.

ELIZA. America says that we colored people have to ride in the front car of the train.

MICHAEL. How many times you rode the train north?

ELIZA. Many times.

MICHAEL. And you know where you suppose to sit? Right?

ELIZA. Where I want to sit.

MICHAEL. Then let's go back up there and take the first seats we see.

ELIZA. Son, I am sixty-five years old. I have worked in my restaurant for near thirty years. And you know, there is only one kind of person I want in my place, and that's a decent person. Everyone is welcome.

MICHAEL. Mrs...

ELIZA. Watkins.

MICHAEL. You know your place. But your place is not ours. *(Pointing to Sadie and Frank).*

ELIZA. I'm tired of this talking. I want to read my Bible. Sadie bring me my Bible.

SADIE. *(Pointing to her seat)* It's over there Mama.

ELIZA. Bring it to me child. *(Sadie walks over and gets the Bible and gives it to her)* You see this Bible here. You, me, everyone, is going to have to give account of everything we do down here. The Lord will judge us all, colored and white. I am not the judge. The scripture says "Judge not! So ye be not judged." The white man has to meet the master one day. That's all I have to say. *(She sits).*

FRANK. *(Waits until Eliza takes her seat)* But, there is no reason why we should have to ride in such a hot place.

MICHAEL. Boiling. *(He loosens his collar).*

FRANK. Boiling. Whatever! Yeah. You're right. I don't want to be here.

MICHAEL. Then let's get out of here.

SADIE. Don't listen to him Frank.

MICHAEL. You want this whole train of GI's to know you caved in to that conductor? He barely went past the eighth grade.

FRANK. Of course not!

MICHAEL. Then stand up like a Marine.

ELIZA. Listen boys. Let's sing a song.

FRANK. I ain't in no mood for singing.

ELIZA. You need to sing. It's good for your soul.

MICHAEL. Singing?

ELIZA. *(Looking at Mike)* You need to sing more than he does.

MICHAEL. Mam. I thought long and hard before I came in here.

ELIZA. Did you pray?

MICHAEL. No mam, I'm not religious.

ELIZA. But you need to ask for some strength, from the Lord.

MICHAEL. I meditated last night.

ELIZA. You need to sing a song of Zion. A song to uplift your spirit. Cause you need a lot of uplifting. You need the Holy Ghost to come into your soul. To take out all that pride. All that anger.

MICHAEL. I got a right to be angry for what they did to Frank.

ELIZA. But can you break man's law because you are angry? There is a more perfect law.

MICHAEL. If I don't see it, I don't believe it.

ELIZA. Son. You need to pray.

FRANK. Mike. Go back!

MICHAEL. Not without you.

FRANK. Now! *(Mike starts to walk slowly out).*

ELIZA. We all need to sing. Singing lightens your heart. Eases your burdens. *(She sings a spirited gospel song—one by Mahalia Jackson. As she finished her song, Sadie and Frank settle into their seats and the lights slowly fade).*

Scene III

This scene, which is Frank's dream, opens outside the train. The lights are dimly lit. You can hear a voice calling repeatedly "Frank Bispham." The call gets louder and louder, then we see Frank rise slowly from a sleep, clothed in his Marine uniform.

FRANK. Yes sir. Yes sir. I'm Frank. I was getting ready. *(He looks around and no one is there.)* I'm ready now. *(Scott, the white conductor walks on stage clothed in a Marine captain's uniform jacket and a German helmet).*

SCOTT. Attention! *(Frank snaps to attention)* Your name boy!

FRANK. Private Frank Bispham, sir!

SCOTT. Straighten up your tie boy!

FRANK. Yes sir. Yes sir. *(He frantically straightens his tie).*

SCOTT. Can I see my face in those boots boy? *(Frank nervously looks down at his boots)* Straighten up there. A Marine got to have good posture. Look straight ahead. You understand my point boy?

FRANK. Yes sir. I do. I do.

SCOTT. Now I'm going to walk over there and look at those boots. If I can't see my face, you are finished. You understand me boy?

FRANK. Yes. I understand sir. But these shoes. I mean boots ....

You might not be able to see your face in them.

SCOTT. You talking back to me boy? Is that what you doing?

FRANK. No sir. I'm just saying that the boots are...

SCOTT. Are what? Say it! Say it!

FRANK. Say what sir!

SCOTT. You were getting ready to say it. Not me. You were. Now you want me to believe that you can't say it?

FRANK. If I say it. You might. I mean, like, you are very angry sir.

SCOTT. Is that what you think this is boy? Anger? You haven't seen anger.

FRANK. I guess not.

SCOTT. What did you say, boy?

FRANK. May I be dismissed, sir?

SCOTT. No. Not until I say you are finished.

FRANK. Well, am I finished?

SCOTT. Yes, you are. You can walk back into those barracks and take off that uniform and get back to coonville. You hear me, get back with those coons!

FRANK. For what? Why should I do that?

SCOTT. Because I said so. This war can be won without niggers.

FRANK. Well, I'm not a nigger, sir. I'm a Marine. And I'm going to fight.

SCOTT. Fight. What you know about fighting? We won't win this war by flashing razors at Hitler's throat. Hitler is a man. You must fight him like a man.

FRANK. I've never had a razor in my hand sir. Throughout my entire life

SCOTT *(Reaches into his pocket).* Here's your opportunity. Take this razor and let's see how you fight.

FRANK. No sir. I won't.

SCOTT. You disobeying my order, boy?

FRANK. I won't pick up that razor.

SCOTT. But you want to fight. Let's see what you can do.

FRANK. No. I won't.

SCOTT. Take it, I said! Goddamit, you either take it or I'll blow your fucking head off. *(He takes out a German Lugar and points it at*

Frank) You want to be a man. Let's see how this razor stands up to this Lugar. I'm gonna count to 5 and on 5 I'm gonna blow your head off.

FRANK. Why you doing this, captain?

SCOTT. Because this is war. *(He counts)* One!

FRANK. I don't have a fight with you. We are both Marines.

SCOTT. Wrong boy. I'm a Marine. You're a nigger. *(Counts)* Two!

FRANK. No. I'm an American!

SCOTT. You're a jungle bunny. A coon. And you know what? I'm a coon catcher. That's my job to round up the coons. And I got a pack of dogs out there. Can't you hear them barking. *(Makes barking noise).* They coming your way. They coming after you. *(Counts)* Three!

FRANK. O.K. O.K. Let me have the razor. *(He takes a step forward, then stops)* I can't do this. What am I going to do with the razor?

SCOTT. Kill me. Can you kill me, nigger? How can you kill Hitler and his men, if you can't kill me? Can you kill a white man, nigger? Can you violate this white skin *(Pulls open his shirt)* and make it all red with my white blood? Can you do that, nigger?

FRANK. No. I can't. I can't. I won't take the razor. No. I won't. *(He begins to cry and bend down under the weight of emotions).*

SCOTT. You're a coward, nigger. A Marine has to be able to kill. To snap a man's neck in two, like a chicken or a carrot, with his bare hands. *(Snaps a carrot. Then there is silence).*

FRANK. No. I can't do it.

SCOTT. You are a coward, nigger.

FRANK. No. I'm not. I'm not a coward..

SCOTT. Coward! You are. A Marine can't be a coward! *(Counts)* Four! *(He moves closer to Frank. Puts the gun to his forehead).* It's your last chance boy. Do you want to be a man?

FRANK. If I take the knife, you'll shoot me!

SCOTT. Those are the chances you take. But if you don't take the knife, your fate is the same.

FRANK. Then why should I help you kill me?

SCOTT. Because you want to be a man! Men are not afraid of dying. What's there to be afraid of?

FRANK. I'm not afraid of dying. But this is ridiculous. O.K. O.K.

Let me think about this a little. Could you just back off a few feet? And take that gun from my head. Please!

SCOTT. Now, you gonna beg. Men don't beg. Boy! They fight back!

FRANK. O.K. O..K. I'll fight. But give me a gun too!

SCOTT *(Starts laughing)* Only men carry guns. You think I'm gonna give you a gun to shoot white men? Here, take this. *(Gives him the razor).*

FRANK *(Holding the razor to his side)* Thanks.

SCOTT. Now. I'm gonna back up five feet and put my Luger in its holster. Then I want you to take me.

FRANK. Take you?

SCOTT. Right. Kill me!

FRANK. Kill you?

SCOTT. Cut my throat.

FRANK. But you got that Luger.

SCOTT. In my holster. That makes it even.

FRANK. I guess it does. Doesn't it? *(He looks at the knife momentarily, then lunges forward with the razor raised in his right hand. The conductor steps to the left, causing Frank to fall to the ground. He pulls his pistol, points the gun and fires into Frank. The lights slowly start to fade as the conductor stands, looking around nervously as if he is looking for more enemy soldiers. The lights fade as he is looking).*

Scene IV

The scene opens at about 6 a.m. the next morning, with Sadie and Eliza standing over Frank, who is coming out of his dream.

SADIE. Frank! Wake up! Wake up! It's six a.m.

FRANK. *(He jumps out of his chair)* What happened? Where am I? *(Looking around fanatically)* What is this place?

SADIE. You were dreaming.

FRANK. Dreaming?

SADIE. Yeah. You must have had a nightmare.

FRANK. Wow! *(Rubbing his forehead)* I did. A bad one. Wow! *(He sits back down).*

ELIZA. We need to get him some tea.

FRANK. No. I'll be alright. Everything was so real.

ELIZA. You must have had a humdinger cause you were yelling something about "Don't..."

SADIE. "Don't shoot." That's what he was saying.

ELIZA. Some tea and some breakfast and you'll feel better. That porter'll be by soon. He usually comes to get our orders around six. I'm gonna wash up a little. You just sit and rest. *(She walks back to her seat and gathers some things).*

FRANK. Thanks, Mrs. Watkins.

ELIZA. Sadie. You been to sleep haven't you? (*As she begins to walk past her).*

SADIE. Yes Mama. (*Sam, the porter enters).*

SAM. Good morning. Good morning. We have just entered North Carolina. Wanted to see if anyone wanted breakfast.

ELIZA. We need three teas please. And one orange juice for my granddaughter.

SAM. Yes mam. Good old hot southern teas.

ELIZA. How about sausage and biscuits?

SAM. Yes, we have all that. And eggs and grits. Here's your ordering card. You just check off what you want and I'll bring it to you. *(Looking at Frank)* Howde, Mr. Marine.

FRANK. Hi.

SADIE. He didn't sleep well last night.

FRANK. How far along are we?

SAM. Another 50 miles to your stop in Rockymount. You take a bus from there.

FRANK. Good.

SAM. How about some breakfast?

FRANK. The club car is that way? *(He stands).*

SAM. No. I'll take your order.

FRANK. I think I want to stretch my legs.

SAM. It's off limits.

FRANK. I see. (*He thinks*) You got muffins?

SAM. Biscuits.

FRANK. Biscuits?

SADIE. That's what people eat in the South.

FRANK. O.K., biscuits.

SAM. Check off what you want. *(Gives Frank and Sadie cards. He waits for a while, expecting them to give the cards back to him. They don't give him the cards. He then writes their orders on a card he has in his hand.)* I think I got everything. Three hot teas, one orange juice, biscuits and grits. I'll be seeing you all in a jiffy.

ELIZA. Thank you very much. Remember. I want my tea black. No sugar, no cream. And hot. Don't bring no lukewarm stuff here.

SADIE. And some real grits this time. Hominy.

SAM. I'll get it right. *(He exits).*

FRANK. *(Looking at Sadie)* How about a game of cards? *(Sits down).*

SADIE. *(Sadie goes over and sits with Eliza)* No.

FRANK. No bid whist? (*Looking at Eliza*) You want to play, Mrs. Watkins?

ELIZA. Never touch no cards. No dice. No pool balls. Gambling is a sin against God.

FRANK. You saying I'm a sinner? (*He laughs*) No. It's just clean fun. See, Mrs. Watkins. Clean fun. No money on the table.

SADIE. That's the way we been brought up.

FRANK. Sounds silly to me.

SADIE. Pardon me?

FRANK. I meant to say. I never heard of such thing.

SADIE. There's probably plenty things you never heard of.

FRANK. You might be right.

ELIZA. You know, young man. The Bible says that a child should honor their elders.

FRANK. Well. I agree with that.

ELIZA. You do?

FRANK. Yes, mam. It's the way I was brought up.

ELIZA. Then don't do the devil's work in my presence.

FRANK. What work?

SADIE. The cards, Frank. You should put them away.

FRANK. Put them away? It is only a game.

SADIE. They are sinful, Frank.

ELIZA. I seen too many men get shot and cut up over those cards. I never let em in my house. These hands will never touch em.

FRANK. *(Begins to shuffle the deck)* No problem. *(Just as he starts talking, Michael Cooper enters. Frank doesn't see him. Eliza does).*

ELIZA. Frank. Oh Frank.

FRANK. *(Looks down the isle)* Heah, Mike. *(He gets up and walks toward MIKE).*

MICHAEL. Frank. *(They embrace).*

SADIE. *(Looking at Mike)* Hi, Mike.

MICHAEL. Hi. Everybody.

MICHAEL. Frank. I been talking to myself all day and all night. And I decided....*(Sits next to Eliza).*

ELIZA. How you do? We just ordered some breakfast. Would you like some?

MICHAEL. That would be right kind of you. But we ate already.

FRANK. I was gonna teach Sadie Bid Whist.

MICHAEL. You got to watch him. He taught me that game and wiped me out.

SADIE. We don't talk about cards here.

MICHAEL. What? Frank just said...

FRANK. Mrs. Watkins is a Southern Baptist.

SADIE. *(Sam enters with trays of food)* Oh look a here. Trouble just walked through that door.

SAM *(Looking around).* Here is the food. And the tea is hot, real hot Mrs. Watkins. I made it special for you.

ELIZA *(Taking her tray)* Thank you.

SAM. Frank, this one is yours. And here are the bills.

FRANK. I'll take them.

ELIZA. Thank you, son.

SAM. Is there anything else I can get for you?

MICHAEL. I'll take some orange juice.

SAM. You will have to order that in the club car, sir.

SADIE. Here, have mine.

MICHAEL *(Taking juice)* Thanks.

ELIZA. Have a little of my biscuit. *(She gives it to Mike as she looks at Sam).*

MICHAEL. Thanks.

SADIE. Here's some jelly and some of my biscuit. Nice and hot.

ELIZA. And this tea ain't hot enough. You have it. *(Gives to Mike).*

MICHAEL. Thanks again. I don't want to eat your food.

ELIZA. We share what we got. It might not be much, but if we got it, you can have it.

SADIE. Yeah, little can become much.

ELIZA. Can you bring me a hot cup of tea next time?

SAM. Yes, I'll go and get one for you right now. I'll be right back. *(He exits).*

FRANK. We done done it now.

SADIE. We just sharing what we got. That's all.

MICHAEL. I didn't like that look on his face.

FRANK. He'll be back.

ELIZA. He better. I want that hot tea.

MICHAEL. You gonna get another chance because here he comes.

ELIZA. He got my tea? *(Sam enters with Eliza's tea and the Scott).*

SCOTT. *(Pointing to Mike)* You leave.

SAM . Here's your tea mam *(Giving it to Eliza).*

ELIZA. Thanks, son.

MICHAEL. I am not leaving without Frank.

SCOTT. I am informing you that you are in violation of the rules and regulations of this carrier and federal and state law.

MICHAEL. What are you going to do? Arrest us?

SCOTT. Exactly that. Sam get the cuffs.

SAM. I have two pairs in my pocket. *(He looks at Mike and Frank in a menacing manner).*

SCOTT. When you were sworn in as Marines, didn't you swear under oath to defend and protect the Constitution of the United States?

MICHAEL. Don't interrogate me. I know what I'm doing.

SCOTT. Are you saying you will not obey my lawful orders?

FRANK. Mr. Conductor, when you told me to leave my friends in the other car, I did. When your flunky Sam said we could not visit the club car again, I said fine. Now, you come here, to this place, and tell us that our friend from over there can't visit here.

SCOTT. That's right. He has to leave.

SAM. And I ain't nobody's flunky. *(Moving toward Frank, but is stopped by Scott).*

FRANK. Then, what are you?

SCOTT. He's an employee of this train, and he is doing his job.

FRANK. What is your job? *(Looking at Sam).* To separate friends *(Turning to Scott)* because of something as silly as the color of my skin. Well, I'm telling you, I won't go along with it. It won't work.

ELIZA. Thank God!

SADIE. It won't work.

FRANK. You hear me. It won't work. I'm no different from you *(Pointing at conductor)* or anyone else. Not only is he staying here, if that's what he wants, but I'm going back into the other car with my friends and you can do what you think you have to do.

SADIE. *(Walks up to Frank's side)* There's nothing wrong with Mike visiting us here. He's a decent man and we are decent people.

ELIZA. Hallelujah! We God's people. Mister. *(Stands)* We tired of this ugliness. It's an abomination to God. It stinks in his nostrils. And you *(Pointing to Sam)* You should be ashamed of yourself.

FRANK. So you coming with me? *(Looking at Sadie).*

SADIE. Yes. I am. *(They embrace and exit with Mike. Scott follows them, leaving Sam and Eliza on stage).*

SAM *(Looking at Eliza after watching the three leave).* Mrs Watkins, *(Looking despondent)* I'm not quite sure what I should do.

ELIZA. Come here son. *(Sam looks in the direction of the three again, then at Eliza.)*

SAM. Maybe I should have explained the rules to him.

ELIZA. Sit right here. *(She directs Sam to a seat).* Son, in our town of Spartenburg, there's a grocery store called Carson's Groceries. All of us coloreds use to buy our greens, potatoes, corn meal and okra from him. He knew us all by first name. Then one day I saw him in the Ku Klux Klan procession, driving through the colored section with their horns a blasting. They all draped in their white robes. The first car had a big white cross hanging in the front of it. I'll never forget that, my Jesus' cross in the hands of people so full of hate when all he was about was love. We never bought another thing from old man Carson. We drove him out of business. You know it was his old Studebaker that gave him away. He always had it parked in front of his store, and it was the first car in that procession.

SAM. *(He stands.)* I don't know what to do. I got over ten years on this job. Now most people just obey the rules, like you doing.

ELIZA. But you know with the war and everything, people just like a good fight these days.

SAM. But I got children to feed. Not married, but still children.

ELIZA. I understand. They'll eat son. The Lord will see to it. You mark my words. *(Sam starts to walk off the stage).*

SAM. Yes man. I do hear you.

ELIZA. You think hard about what I just said. And you pray. *(He walks off as the lights slowly fade).*

Scene V

The scene opens thirty minutes later. Mike, Frank and Sadie are looking out the window of the whites only car as it comes to a stop.

SCOTT. *(Walking up to them)* We have to pick up some passengers here and get rid of the three of you. *(Pointing at Mike, Sadie and Frank).*

SADIE. What you think they going to do?

MICHAEL. I don't know.

FRANK. Look over there. Who's he talking to?

MICHAEL. Military Police.

SADIE. And they walking this way.

MICHAEL. You think we've taken this too far?

FRANK. We have to stick together.

MICHAEL. I'm sure they'll realize how stupid this whole thing is.

SADIE. They sure talking for a long time.

SAM. *(Walking by)* Look Frank. You're a good kid. Why don't you obey the law and go back front. That's the MP's and they'll be in here soon.

SAM. I've seen them drag many colored guys off the train. And when they get you off, they don't give you a nice comfortable room in the hotel either. They crack heads.

SADIE. You think they'll do that to him?

SAM. You can count on it.

FRANK. They still talking out there. Mike, what you think?

MICHAEL. What you think?

FRANK. Me?

MICHAEL. Yeah, you.

SAM. Mark my words Frank. Don't give it all up now.

SADIE. They looking over here. Starting to walk toward the train. They got big sticks in their hands.

SAM. That's for your heads.

MICHAEL. So what you say Frank? I'm getting a little scared.

SAM. You should be. I ain't kidding you when I say all they want to do is crack some heads. *(Pointing at Frank)* And especially your head.

SADIE. They getting on the train. What should we do?

MICHAEL. We could just get off and think about it in the station.

FRANK. But that would be giving in to them. Wouldn't it?

SAM. You would be saving your ass.

FRANK. I'm staying on this train. I'm not going into the station and I'm not getting off.

SAM. You crazy.

SADIE. *(Looking at Frank)* Right. We're not leaving. We're staying right here.

SCOTT. *(Entering)* Did you talk some sense into them Sam?

SAM. They say they not leaving. *(Eliza enters and with Bible in hand)*.

ELIZA. I saw the police out the window, and decided to come and witness this. I'm here because I want to be able to speak up about what I see. And I done gave one life, my husband, to this country. And my granddaughter will be the first of our family to enter college. So Mr. conductor if you gonna whip this boy, you got to do it in front of me.

SCOTT. I got the Military Police right here. *(Pointing)* And there's more five minutes away.

ELIZA. I don't want nothing to happen to my granddaughter. You hear me? You hear me Sam?

SAM. She just has to move Mam. And nothing will happen to her.

ELIZA. You hear that dear?

SADIE. I'm not moving, mama.

ELIZA. You know you be starting school in one week. I need you in the restaurant and your mother needs you in Boston. We needs each other baby.

SADIE. *(Standing and going to Eliza)* Fisk can wait. This is something I have to do. Besides I need to ride this train again, when I go back to Boston to check on Mother. I'm not going to breathe all this soot for days, every time I visit my mother.

ELIZA. You heard her, Mr. Conductor. She said she's staying. But you don't have to man-handle her. You hear me! *(The conductor ignores her).* You hear me. *(She shouts again).*

SAM. He hears you, mam.

SADIE *(She stands in front of Mike and Frank)* I'm not a soldier. I'm a civilian. You have no right to touch me. I do have rights. *(She looks Scott in the eyes).*

ELIZA. No, daughter, don't do that. Take your seat.

SADIE. Mama, I must stand here.

FRANK. Sadie.

ELIZA. *(Walks up in front of the conductor)* Mr. Conductor, my husband went into the Army to fight in the First War. Two days later, he was dead. His soul lost. But at least he served, even though it cost him his life. We must be willing to sacrifice in this life, in order to gain a better life. To get to these children, you got to get through me. You gonna have those police beat an old colored woman. Now that wouldn't look good for you and your train, would it?

SADIE. If you touch my grandma, I'll tear you *(Pointing at Conductor)* and this train apart.

SCOTT. Don't you threaten me. Don't you....Cause I'll..

SADIE. Cause you'll what?

SCOTT. You'll see what?

FRANK. No one is going to get beaten here. (*Stands*).

MICHAEL. Last I heard our enemy was Germany and Japan. (*Stands*).

SCOTT. I have worked on this railroad for twenty-three years, right out of school. I got seven children and a wife. This is my job, my livelihood. If I don't work, my kids don't eat. Now I got the Military Police here (*Pointing*) to help me do my job. And by the love of Jesus I'm going to do it. You got those cuffs, Sam?

SAM. Yes sir. I do.

ELIZA. Then Sam, I want to be the first person you put them on. *(She raises her arms in front of Sam, holding the Bible in one hand. There is a hesitation).*

SCOTT. Go ahead Sam. Do your job. *(There is silence. Sam looks ELIZA in the eyes).*

SAM. Sir, I can put them on the soldiers. Not her. *(There is silence).*

SCOTT. She is interfering with the operation of this train.

SAM. But sir. She's a lady! A Christian lady at that!

SCOTT. Are you disobeying my orders too. Because if you are, maybe you should write me a letter of resignation, this minute. Are you disobeying me?

SAM. No. I'm not sir. *(Turns to Eliza)* I'm sorry mam, but its my living. *(He cuffs her, the Bible falls to the floor).*

FRANK. What are you doing? *(Yelling and moving toward Sam. The conductor steps between him and Sam. Sadie runs up to Sam and starts beating him in the chest with her fists).*

SADIE. (*Picking up the Bible*) Let my Mama go. No! (*Screams at the top of her voice*).

FRANK. *(Grabs her)* Sadie. Sadie. I'll handle it. (*He pushes her behind him. She is crying*) Let her go. (*Looking at the Conductor*).

MICHAEL. You won't get away with that! *(Looking at Conductor)* And you'll be next. *(Pointing at Sam).*

SAM. You don't scare me. All you had to do was obey the law.

FRANK. You're a disgrace!

SAM. No! I'm an employee! Do you have a job now?

SCOTT. This train will not leave until you three get off!

FRANK. Take the cuffs off her. This wasn't her fight.

SCOTT. Only if you leave.

SADIE. We'll leave. We don't want no part of your train. Get your filthy hands off my Mama. You got no right to touch her. *(Cries, Frank embraces her)*.

FRANK. O.K. We'll. We'll leave. Take them off.

SCOTT. You promise that you will leave my train?

SADIE. Yes. We promise. Just take them off!

SCOTT. Take em off Sam.

SAM. Yes sir. *(He removes cuffs)*.

FRANK. Let's get off this thing. *(He puts his arms around Sadie)*.

SADIE. *(Turning to Grandma.)* I love you mama. And I appreciate everything you've done.

ELIZA. You are a good girl Sadie.

SADIE. Mama, I've tried to do what you want me to do.

ELIZA. You don't have to get off baby. We're almost home now. Come with me.

SADIE. But Mama, I'm with friends.

ELIZA. It's alright baby. It's alright.

SADIE. It is?

ELIZA. Yes. It is. The Lord is with you.

SADIE. *(Turning to Frank)* O.K., O.K., Let's go.

ELIZA. I'm going back to my seat. I got some scriptures to read. *(She exits to the front of the train)*.

FRANK *(Looking at Scott)*. You may have won this battle.

MICHAEL. We're soldiers. Fighting is what we get paid to do.

SCOTT. I get paid for this job too.

ELIZA *(Returns)*. Here take my Bible. *(Gives to Sadie)*.

SADIE. Thanks Mama *(Sobbing)*. I'll bring it back to you. *(Eliza exits)*. Let's get off this train. *(Looking at Frank)*.

FRANK. So long Sam and Mr. Conductor. I didn't want to ride your train anyway. Sam, don't ever get on a train when you don't know where it's going. Good bye. *(Frank exits with Mike and Sadie)*.

SCOTT. You boys go. I got my train back. And you're wrong. We know exactly where its headed. Sam let's go have a drink.

SAM. Not right now sir. Maybe later. I surely need one. But not now. *(Lights out).*

Scene VI

This scene opens thirty minutes later with Mike and Sadie standing outside in front of a bus stop.

MICHAEL. The busses leave from here every half an hour. You have to go to Charlotte, then change for a bus to Spartenburg.

SADIE. How many miles are we from Spartenburg?

MICHAEL. I'm not sure. But I know its quite a ways. I picked up the tickets.

SADIE. Thanks.

MICHAEL. Frank should be getting back here with those sandwiches.

SADIE. How do you feel about everything?

MICHAEL. I never knew I would ever be in a situation like that. Never in my wildest dreams.

SADIE. Neither did I. I can't wait to tell my mother about this.

MICHAEL. So, you are going to Boston?

SADIE. I think so. Nashville is closer to North Carolina, but my mother needs me right now. So, I'll postpone my enrollment to Fisk for a year. Go back to Boston to help her wind down her business. Then, who knows. One thing's for sure, I feel freer than I have ever felt in my life.

MICHAEL. You know, I'm sorry not knowing anything about Fisk. And I did read *The Souls of Black Folk.* You're right. Du Bois did graduate from Fisk before Harvard.

SADIE. Neither of us knew anything about each other.

MICHAEL. We learned a lot today.

SADIE. And that's for sure. I never met anyone like Frank before.

MICHAEL. He is quite a character

SADIE. You will stay in touch with him?

MICHAEL. You can count on it. *(Frank enters).*

SADIE. You get the sandwiches?

FRANK. Yeah. But that place is something else.

SADIE. Crowded?

FRANK. I go to the bus station cafeteria and all the white people are sitting, eating.

SADIE. Oh, I should have told you.

FRANK. I'm sitting there and not getting served. And getting hot.

SADIE. You been hot enough.

MICHAEL. That's for sure.

FRANK. So I ask the lady if I could get some service and she pointed to a line.

MICHAEL. Did you get in the line?

FRANK. I had to. All the coloreds were standing up outside the cafeteria ordering through a window on the street.

SADIE. You went outside, didn't you?

FRANK. I had to. The same waitress waited on me.

MICHAEL. At the window.

FRANK. Yeah. This place is going to be one experience.

SADIE. Don't worry. You'll learn quick.

MICHAEL. I got a lot of learning to do too.

FRANK. Here. I bought three Dr. Peppers and three greasy cheeseburgers.

SADIE. (*Taking her food.*) I'm going to run and catch the bus. It leaves in ten minutes for Spartenburg. Frank, you got my address. We'll get together.

FRANK *(Putting down his food)* Thanks for standing with us Sadie. Let me know how your mother is doing.

SADIE. I'll write you everyday. And when you get back from the war, I'll be at either Fisk, Blessed Barbecue, or Weezie's Beauty Salon.

FRANK. I'll look for those letters, everyday. (*They embrace*).

SADIE. (*Starting to move off-stage*) So I'll see you Michael. Next time we'll play bid whist. (*Slowly walks off stage*).

MICHAEL. We better get moving.

FRANK. Why the rush?

MICHAEL. While you were getting the food, I got the tickets.

FRANK. We don't leave right away, do we?

MICHAEL. No. We got some time.

FRANK. Let's sit before we get on the bus. *(They sit on their duffle bags).*

MICHAEL. Wait until I write my father about this. I'm glad to be off that train, but this is not right. The war won't be the same.

FRANK. Neither will I.

MICHAEL. That's for sure. And I'll write.

FRANK. You better, cause I want my book. How could you leave it on the train? *(Laughs).*

MICHAEL. I'll get it when I get in North Carolina. But only if you promise that your Mom will send me some more of those fish cakes.

FRANK. When we come home from the war, you can visit us in Cambridge and eat fish cakes all night.

MICHAEL. That sounds good. *(They laugh. Lights begin to fade).*

FRANK. And we can throw a party and calypso to the wee hours of the night. And of course, Sadie will be there. *(Lights continue to fade).*

MICHAEL. Sounds like a plan. *(Lights black out).*

END OF PLAY

Chronology

1948   (May 13), Born in Summit, TN, USA., to Robert C. Johnson, Sr. of Ooltewah, TN and Louise Burgan of Summit, TN

1950   Family moves to Boston, Massachusetts. Lives in Black neighborhood (South End of Boston, Roxbury and Mattapan).

1952   (To 1958) Attends the Dwight (Elementary) School in the South End of Boston.

1959   (To 1960) Attends Charles E. Mackey Middle School in the South End of Boston.

1961   (To 1965) Attends the Commonwealth School, a private day school in the Back Bay of Boston on scholarship.

1966   (Summer) Counselor, Thompson's Academy of Upward Bound Program, sponsored by government and private colleges and designed to stimulate academic motivation in youngsters from lower economic communities.

1967   Earns the Diploma of the Commonwealth School, Massachusetts.
(Summer) Youth worker, United South End Settlements; counseled teenagers in the Black Community of Boston, working out of the oldest social service organization in Boston.

1968   First play, *Coffee and Sour Cream*, completed and produced at Bowdoin College, Brunswick, Maine and in Boston.
(Summer) Community Worker in Nigeria, in the program, "Experiment in International Living": lived and worked in a small village outside Ibadan, helping in the construction of a village post office.

1969   (Summer) Youth Worker, United South End Settlements.

1970   (Summer) Counselor and Instructor in Afro-American History in the Boston College Upward Bound Program.

1971   (January-September) Serves as Counselor in the Manpower Training Program of the Boston Architectural Center.
(June) Graduates with a BA degree in Government and Legal Studies from Bowdoin College.
Wins the Thomas J. Watson Fellowship for play writing in

East Africa and England. Sojourned in Tanzania, Ethiopia, Kenya and Nigeria.

1972 (February). Second play, *Mama's Boy*, completed. Premiere performance by Kenya National Theatre, directed by Tirus Gathwe.

(Summer) Serves as Instructor in Black History in the University of Massachusetts at Boston Upward Bound Program.

1973 (Summer) Participates in a two-week seminar on "The Humanist Tradition" held at Aspen Institute for Humanistic Studies (Colorado); works in the legal section of the First National Bank of Boston for ten weeks.

1974 (Summer) teaches African History to Black freshmen at Brandeis University in a six-week summer program called "special services".

1975 Obtains the Masters in Professional Studies (MPS) degree in African and Afro-American Studies from Cornell University.

(Summer) "Master Teacher" in the Upward Bound Program of Brandeis University, teaching a seminar on "Survival Techniques in Black Literature."

(September 1975 to June 1976) Serves as part-time Instructor in History, Ithaca College, Ithaca, New York.

1976 (April) Six photographs published in *Watu*, Black Literary Magazine of Cornell University.

(September 1976 to June 1978) Serves as part-time Instructor in Business Law, Roxbury Community College, Boston, Massachusetts.

1977 (April) Thirteen photographs published in Cornell Law Forum.

(June) Earns the Doctor of Laws (JD) degree from the Cornell Law School.

(June, to June 1978) Serves as Director of Affirmative Action, Massachusetts Board of Regional Community Colleges.

1978 (June, to June 1982) Serves as Director of Affirmative Action, University of Massachusetts at Boston.

(September, to June 1981) Serves as Part-time Instructor in Law, Black Studies, and Law and Justice, University of

Massachusetts at Boston.
1980 (To 1982) Host, "From the Source", a weekly radio talk-show, WUMB-FM 91.9, Boston, Massachusetts.
1981 (September 1981 to June 1992) Serves as part-time Instructor in the Public Administration Program, Northeastern University, Boston.
(September 1981 to June 1982) Serves as part-time Visiting Assistant Professor in African and Afro-American Studies, Brandeis University, Waltham, Massachusetts,
1982 (June, to June 1985) Joins the law firm, Salgo and Lee of Boston, Massachusetts, as Counsel.
(September, to June 1984) Serves as full-time Assistant Professor in Law at Bentley College.
(December) Photographs published in the book, *Understanding the African Philosophical Concept Behind the "Diagram of the Law of Opposites"* by Dr. Yosef Ben-Jochannan, Evelyn Walker, Dorothy Lee Cobb, and Calvin Birdsong.
Serves in the United States Office of Personnel Management.
1983 Serves in the Editorial Board of WNEV-TV, Boston.
1985 (June, to December 1989) Runs own firm, Law Offices of Robert Johnson, Jr., Boston, Massachusetts.
1990 (January, to September 1990) Runs the firm, Johnson and Jenkins, Attorneys at Law, Boston, Massachusetts, as Partner.
1991 Third play. *Sugar Hill*, co-authored with Amy Merrill (Ansara). Premiere performance by Karibu Productions or Erhlich Theatre, March 14-April 17, directed by William Electric Black.
1993 Rejoins the Department of Black Studies (now Africana Studies Department), University of Massachusetts at Boston, as a part-time assistant professor (to May 1994).
Serves as Visiting Associate Professor at Wellesley College (to May 1994).
1994 Fourth play, *Freedom's Journeyman*, co-authored with Amy Merrill. Premiere performance staged as part of Bowdoin College's Bicentennial Celebrations, March 4-6, directed by Nefertiti Burton.

September. Formally joins the Black Studies Department as Full-time Assistant Professor in the Department of Africana Studies, University of Massachusetts at Boston.

World premiere of fifth play, *Stop and Frisk*, presented by Karibu Productions at the Strand Theatre, Columbia Road, Dorchester, Massachusetts, November 25-27, directed by James A. Spruill, following successful staged reading at the Playwrights Platform's Annual Summer Festival of New Plays, Massachusetts College of Art, in June.

1995 Play, *Mama's Boy*, published in International Journal of Black Drama, Volume 1 (Temple University, Philadelphia).

1996 (February) Twenty photographs of the "Million Man March" featured in a show at the Harbor Gallery, University of Massachusetts at Boston.

1997 First scholarly work for younger readers, *Shona*, co-authored with Gary N. van Wyck, published in its *Heritage Library of African Peoples* by the Rosen Publishing Group, New York.

1998 First edition of second scholarly work, *Race, Law and Public Policy: Cases and Materials on Law and Public Policy of Race*, published in Baltimore by Black Classic Press.

Staged reading of sixth play, *The Train Ride*, directed by James A. Spruill, presented at the Playwrights' Platform, Massachusetts College of Art Auditorium, Wednesday June 10, as part of the 1998 Summer Festival of New Plays.

1999 (May) Three photographs feature in CD *Mingo* released by Third Degree Records; Two phonographs published in Worcester Gazette..

(October) *The Train Ride* presented in workshop by Cambridge Multicultural Arts Center (October 1) and at the University of Massachusetts Boston (October 22).

Third scholarly work, *Why Blacks Left America for Africa*, published in New York by Praeger.

2000 Fourth scholarly work, *Returning Home: A Century of African-American Repatriation*, completed and accepted for publication.

September. Begins sabbatical leave (as Visiting Scholar) at

Vanderbilt University, Tennessee.
2001 Granted tenure and promoted to the rank of Associate Professor in the Department of Africana Studies, University of Massachusetts at Boston..
(January). Completes sabbatical leave at Vanderbilt University, Tennessee.
(February) *The Train Ride* presented in workshop at American Theatre of Actors, New York City.
(September). Assumes Chairmanship of the Africana Studies Department, University of Massachusetts at Boston.
2002 Second edition of *Race, Law and Public Policy: Cases and Materials on Law and Public Policy of Race*, published in Baltimore by Black Classic Press.
2003 January. *Two Plays of Initiation* (Stop and Frisk and The Train Ride) published by Nsibidi Africana Publishers, Milton, USA and London, England.

Glossary

ADAMS STREET: A main street running through the Orchard Housing Project, Roxbury, Massachusetts.

BID WHIST: A card game popular among blacks in the United States of America.

CAMP LEJEUNE: A segregated boot camp for US Black Marines.

CHIPPIES: Black American slang for young, attractive girl or woman.   Dominican

CHITTLINS: Hog intestines eaten by many Southern US Blacks.

COLTRANE, JOHN: An African-American musician, widely recognized as the greatest Saxophone Jazz player.

COONS: A derogatory term for Blacks in the United States, especially those Blacks that ape White American mannerisms.

COONVILLE: From COON (above), a derogatory designation of the Black community.

DAVIDOFFS: Fine Dominican cigars.

DIDDLEY: African-American slang for "absolutely".

FISK UNIVERSITY: A well-known historically-black university, located in Nashville, Tennessee.

FLYNN, RAY: Mayor of the City of Boston (1984-1993).

GERMAN LUGAR: Military pistol used by Germans.

HIGH YELLA: African-American slang for a very light-complexioned Black person.

HOMINY: A brand of grits, a breakfast cereal popular among southern African-Americans.

HUMDINGER: In African-American slang, a person not to be believed in or trusted.

JACKSON, MAHALIA: Preeminent African-American Gospel singer.

MASON-DIXON LINE: The line that separates the southern slave states from the northern free states.

MESSENGILL, JAMES: A fictional character.

MONTFORD POINT: The city in North Carolina where CAMP LEJEUNE (*op. cit.*) is located.

ORCHARD PARK PROJECTS: A public housing complex located near Dudley in Roxbury, Massachusetts.

POONTANG: African-American slang for the female genitalia.

RANDOLPH, A. PHILIP: Founder and President of the Brotherhood of Sleeping Car Porters.

ROXBURY: A district of the City of Boston, Massachusetts; the heart of the city's black community.

SCROUNGEY: In African-American slang, unattractive and skinny.

STUDEBAKER: A brand of automobile that was popular in the 1940's.

VANDROSS, LUTHER: An African-American Soul singer.

WASHINGTON, DENZEL: Preeminent African-American actor.

WHEN I HAD LAY OVERS: An African-American idiom for "when I stayed overnight."

WILLIAMS, BILLY DEE: An African-American actor.

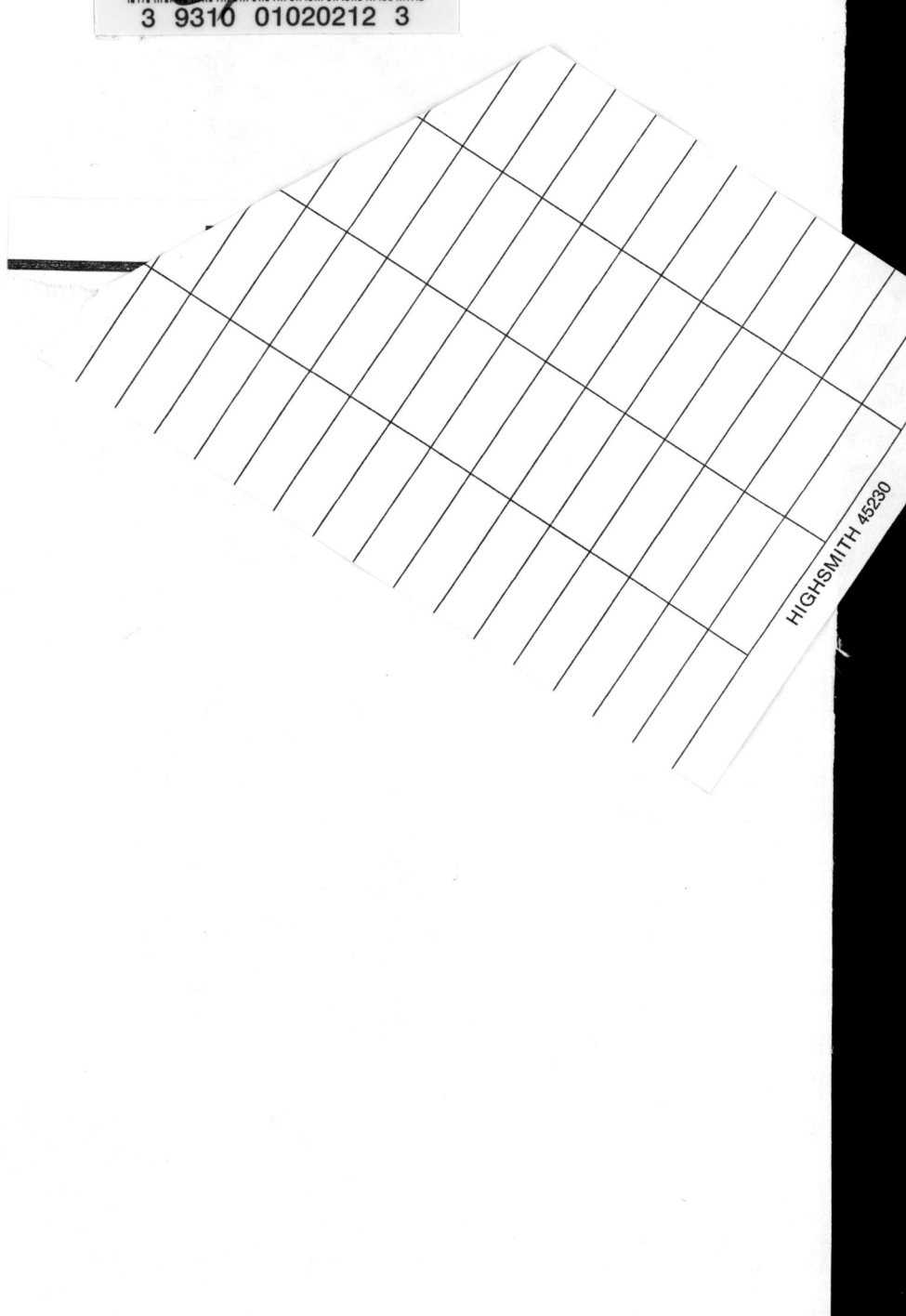